THE NATIONAL PALACE, SINTRA

THE NATIONAL PALACE, SINTRA

JOSÉ CUSTÓDIO VIEIRA DA SILVA

MINISTÉRIO DA CULTURA

INSTITUTO
PORTUGUÊS DO
PATRIMÓNIO
ARQUITECTÓNICO

© Instituto Português do Património Arquitectónico (IPPAR)
and Scala Publishers, 2002

First published in 2002 by Scala Publishers Ltd
Gloucester Mansions
140a Shaftesbury Avenue
London WC2H 8HD

Designed by Anikst Design
Publication Coordinator (IPPAR): Dulce de Freitas Ferraz
Collaboration (IPPAR): Isabel Lage, Henrique Ruas
Translated from the Portuguese by Gilla Evans
Edited by Slaney Begley
Printed and bound in Spain by A. G. Elkar, S. Coop.

ISBN 1 85759 181 X

Photographic credits:
All the photographs are by Luís Pavão
Except: IPPAR/Henrique Ruas: pp. 29 (13), 36, 77 (63), 82, 88, 91, 97, 122, 124, 125
IAN/TT: pp. 31, 65, 71

Plans: © IPPAR/Atelier Santa-Ritta, Architects

ACKNOWLEDGEMENTS

I would like to thank the President and Vice-President of IPPAR, Instituto Português do
Património Arquitectónico, for their kind invitation to write this book on the National Palace
of Sintra. I would also like to express my thanks to its Director, Dr Inês Ferro, and to her
colleagues for their helpfulness and understanding in providing access to the palace – the many
talks we have had have helped me to match the tour itineraries more closely with the historical
development of the building.

The National Palace of Sintra is examined here only in terms of its architecture and history. It
has not been my intention to consider the (very many) objects that are on exhibit in its rooms,
because none of them are original to the palace. This will be the task of another book altogether.
I eagerly await the study of various very fine items that are part of the heritage of this building
and that have been completely disregarded until recently. These will one day, following the dedicated and skilled work of the palace's technical staff, provide an added dimension to a visit to
the palace. This work will not only enhance the reputation of the National Palace of Sintra but
also will enrich our knowledge of the history of art in Portugal.

José Custódio Vieira da Silva

CONTENTS

FOREWORD

The National Palace of Sintra is one of Portugal's most frequently visited monuments – and for good reason. The palace at Sintra is one of the most famous royal residences of medieval Europe; it is also one of the most well-preserved. Parts remain of the mid-fourteenth-century palace – including significant buildings commissioned by Dom João I – as do the successive additions made to it in the fifteenth century, during the reigns of Dom Duarte and Dom Afonso V.

But it was the reign of Dom Manuel that brought the most magnificent extensions to the palace, and its present layout is due in large measure to the work of this king. Dom Manuel, continuing a longstanding tradition of his ancestors, paid particular attention to what was known as the 'Luso-Moorish' style, referred to in the language of art history as Mudéjar art. It is this Mudéjar spirit that puts the palace at Sintra in a class of its own as a building, for the structure contains innumerable evocations of Arab architecture. These are found in the arrangement of the spaces, the inclusion of interior courtyards, the ubiquitous presence of water – forming mirrors, fountains and jets – and of course the great panels of geometric glazed tiles that line its walls.

It is the interplay of intimacy and the representation of power (so clearly stated in the imposing Sala dos Brasões), and the skilful combination of 'interior' and 'exterior' that make the National Palace of Sintra one of the most original examples of the private architecture of royalty. On days when Sintra is not foggy and humid, the conical chimneys of the palace stand out in dazzling contrast against a clear, deep blue sky. They indicate the work of humankind amidst a range of hills that was described by the poet and dramatist Gil Vicente as a true 'garden of Earthly Paradise'.

Luis Ferreira Calado

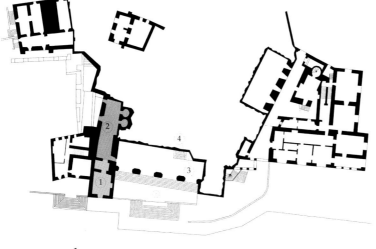

FLOOR 1

1 Toilets
2 Tickets and Shop
3 Entrance
4 Exit

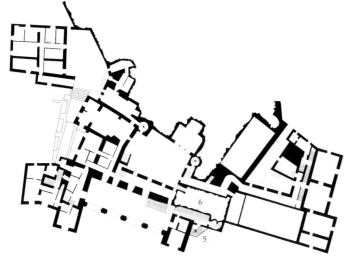

FLOOR 2

5 Entrance Corridor
6 Exit

FLOOR 3

7 Sala dos Archeiros
8 Kitchen
9 Sala da Coroa
10 Sala de César
11 Sala de Dom Sebastião
12 Sala das Sereias
13 Sala das Pegas
14 Sala dos Cisnes

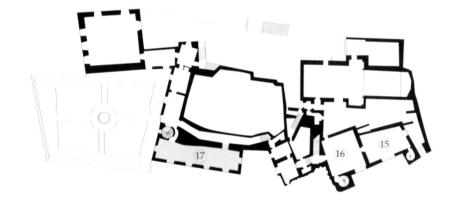

FLOOR 4

15 Quarto de Hóspedes
16 Sala dos Árabes
17 Sala das Galés

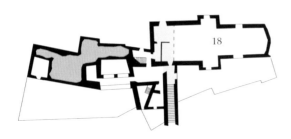

FLOOR 5

18 Chapel

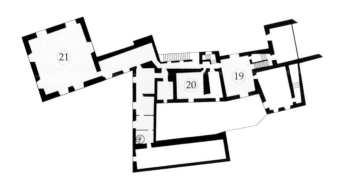

FLOOR 6

19 Sala Chinesa
20 Quarto de Dom Afonso VI
21 Sala dos Brasões

PERIODS OF CONSTRUCTION

The National Palace of Sintra, more commonly known as the Palácio da Vila (Town Palace) – to differentiate it from the nineteenth-century Pena Palace, which looks down upon it haughtily from its mountain stronghold – is an exceptional building in Portugal, both in terms of its history and its architecture. In fact, of the many palaces that the Portuguese monarchy built or took over in various parts of the country during the Middle Ages, the palace at Sintra is the only example to survive with its medieval architectural form almost intact. All the others – and there were many – have either been lost completely, swept away by the tides of history, or have been transformed so extensively that it is virtually impossible to analyse or understand them clearly in terms of their medieval origins.

The only other royal palace that is comparable to the palace at Sintra is the palace at Leiria, built by Dom João I (1357–1433) in the precincts of Leiria Castle and incorporating a section of the city walls. Although it is possible to determine the basic outline of its buildings and the organization of its principal spaces, the major restoration and almost total reconstruction carried out by E. Korrodi in the early twentieth century limits its historical value and to some extent its credibility, in this context, in comparison with what can be seen in the palace at Sintra.

The medieval palaces that belonged to the Portuguese monarchy are not the only ones to have been destroyed: those owned by other members of the aristocracy and the higher clergy almost all suffered the same fate. Either they have been lost to us altogether, ruined or totally transformed, or they have undergone such extensive restoration in the twentieth century – the most glaring example of this being the palace of the dukes of Bragança in Guimarães – that any serious and convincing historical analysis that might have been made of what remains of the medieval roots of their architecture is seriously undermined.

All these factors lend support to our initial claim that the National Palace of Sintra stands as a unique example of medieval architecture. Indeed, the state of conservation of this building's structures and principles of space not only provides the art historian with a living example of how the main internal and external spaces of the homes of the medieval nobility – the so-called palaces – were organized and arranged, and even the functions each of these spaces performed, but also gives an idea of the daily life that went on in them during that long period known as the Middle Ages, particularly during its final moments (the fifteenth and sixteenth centuries).

But the importance of the National Palace of Sintra does not lie solely in its being the only remaining medieval example of the property of the Portuguese monarchy. Its genuinely original architecture finds no easy parallel with any other European palace of the same era. Also, its age and continuity of use have resulted in it being the scene of a great many significant events in Portugal's history, making it a silent but living witness to this history. Finally, its very location at the foot of a mountain, which for thousands of years has been a place of mythical and sacred rites and

2. The mountains and town and of Sintra viewed from the veranda of the palace's Manueline Wing

3. Sala dos Brasões seen from a palace window

cosmogonic interpretations, gives it a highly poetic aura that adds to its fascination and amplifies its sense of mystery.

The history of the National Palace of Sintra begins during the Arab dominion over the Iberian Peninsula, when the *alcaides* (Moorish governors) of Lisbon decided to build two fortresses on a mountain close to the great city. The first was on the top of the mountain and mimicked in its unusual profile the cluster of craggy rocks on which it stood – even today it goes by the poetic name of Castelo dos Mouros (Moors' Castle). Its function was strictly military: it offered an observation point over the ocean and served to protect the city of Lisbon itself. The second fortress, at the foot of the same mountain, was intended for repose and the enjoyment of nature, particularly during the intense heat of summer. The testimony of the Arab geographer Al-Bacr, written in the tenth century, is categorical in this respect: 'Sintra has two castles of extreme solidity' (see A. Borges Coelho, *Portugal na Espanha Árabe*, 1971–4).

This description certainly fits the Castelo dos Mouros, but Al-Bacr's reference to a second castle has produced a certain amount of debate among historians keen to interpret his words correctly. Close and careful examination of the site on which the National Palace of Sintra is built, however, is enough to clear up any confusion. It is indeed a rocky hill – a genuine acropolis – that, particularly on the east side, benefits from a sudden drop, providing a natural defence and, therefore, a suitable site for a military structure. For a long time the palace itself had a circuit of walls and a tall tower that confirmed its primary purpose as castle or fortress, but that contained within it a grand residence in the manner typical of the Islamic citadel. It is surely to this that the geographer Al-Bacr refers in his assertion of the existence of two castles at Sintra.

In 1147, when the first king of Portugal, Afonso Henriques (c.1109–85), conquered the important city of Lisbon, Sintra saw no point in resistance and surrendered immediately. This led to the initial occupation of the fertile Sintra lands by the new Christian conquerors, in a process that was encouraged by the king himself who, in 1154, granted these early occupiers an advantageous land charter. However, Dom Afonso Henriques kept the palaces of the Moorish governors for the Portuguese crown. The palace at Sintra's excellent position on the outskirts of Lisbon was an asset that was sure to have been appreciated by the Portuguese king. Indeed, these palaces within Moorish fortresses, normally located in cities and inhabited by regional *alcaides*, generally enjoyed high social and political prestige – more than sufficient reason for the Christian kings, both in Portugal and in the rest of the Iberian Peninsula, to ensure that they were normally reserved for themselves, following their conquests.

After this initial period, the early years of Christian life at the palace disappear into a long silence, explained by the ebb and flow of the Reconquest of the territory from the Moors. The first known explicit reference to the palace at Sintra did not occur until over a century later. In 1281 Dom Dinis (1261–1325) granted various privileges to the emancipated Moors of Colares to work in the castle and in the houses of the old fortified town (on the high mountain) and also in the palace (*mea palacia*, in the literal transcription of the relevant document) situated on the soil of Oliva. There is no doubt that this refers to the present National Palace of Sintra or Town Palace.

All this points to it being during the reign of Dom Dinis that the palace was first extended or, at least, was adapted to new needs and requirements reflecting a higher standard of comfort. Other palaces built by the same king are known, as are existing buildings that he refurbished with new facilities, so his intervention on the palace at Sintra accords perfectly well with this policy of entire construction or simple improvement. The area involved in this refurbishment by Dom Dinis certainly included the parts situated in the highest part of the rocky acropolis, notably the chapel, where his hand is particularly conspicuous

5. Central Courtyard,
from the Sala dos Árabes

6. External façade of the
Sala dos Cisnes, the
most important section
of the palace complex
built by Dom João I
(c.1425)

– it is possible that the original construction of the chapel was sponsored by this king. Although some architectural elements remain that can confirm his involvement in the residential part of the palace, because this area underwent subsequent alterations it is harder to identify specific elements attributable, with any historical certainty, to the reign of Dom Dinis.

The second major period of construction of the National Palace of Sintra was the work of the aforementioned Dom João I. Although the exact date of this work is not known, most historians who have dedicated themselves to studying the building agree that the probable period was following the conquest of the town of Ceuta (1415). A building warrant dated 1425, in which the royal accountant Rodrigo Anes refers to the book given to him by Lopo Gonçalves, the works registrar – 'that the said Senhor ordered to be made at Sintra' – appears to confirm this. As a consequence, it is thought that the most grandiose and extensive enlargement that the old Moorish palace has undergone to date was begun ten years after the beginning of Portuguese conquests in Africa.

The intervention of Dom João I was, in fact, profound and very significant. He added to the existing structure a large group of buildings that are built around an internal courtyard – the Pátio Central (Central Courtyard) or Pátio do Esguicho (Fountain Courtyard) – and form an entirely autonomous and separate palace. It can be said that it is this transformation that is really responsible for the image of grandeur and originality that the palace acquired. Beginning with the opulent

kitchen and its monumental and emblematic chimneys, passing through the Sala dos Cisnes (Swan Room), Sala das Pegas (Magpie Room) and Sala das Sereias (Mermaid Room), and finishing in the interior room (known today as the Quarto de Hóspedes or Guest Room), it is these buildings that together make up the essential part of the tour offered to the present-day visitor to the National Palace of Sintra.

There were several reasons for the attention Dom João I lavished upon his residence. Firstly, it reflected the increasing importance being placed upon the residences of the monarchy and nobility all over Europe as symbols of political power and social ranking. Secondly, it satisfied the need the Portuguese monarch felt to assert, through a building such as this, his prestige as the founder of a new dynasty, born accidentally of a political crisis. Finally, its proximity to Lisbon and the richness of its hunting grounds (a sport about which the king was particularly passionate, indeed he wrote a treatise on the technique of riding and hunting on horseback – the *Livro da Montaria*) encouraged Dom João I to put a great deal of effort into the enlargement and embellishment of his palace at Sintra.

It was, furthermore, Dom João I and his successors up to and including Dom Manuel I (1469–1521) who made greatest use of this residence and who contributed the most to the essential appearance it has retained to this day.

Dom Duarte (1391–1438) completed some of the work begun by his father, Dom João I. More important than any physical changes, however, was the marked preference shown by Dom Duarte for the palace at Sintra. Indeed, not only did he leave us a remarkable description of the building, but he also specified, in a letter in his own hand, the reasons that led him to use it with particular regularity. These reasons, because of their value in helping us understand the interest shown by the monarchs in this palace, will be analysed elsewhere in this book. Let it be said, however, that the fact that Dom Duarte's son and successor Dom Afonso V (1432–81) was born here was not mere chance, but the consequence of the high esteem in which the palace was held at this time.

The circumstances of his birth may well have been behind the emotional link felt by Dom Afonso V for the palace at Sintra, a link that is given additional resonance by the fact that it is also here that he died. Although there are no known documents that categorically identify which work was carried out by this king, everything seems to point to the notable Mudéjar ceiling (of Moorish inspiration) of the palace chapel, as well as the extremely important ceramic floor of its chancel, being the result of his initiative. Certainly, he commissioned the artist Nuno Gonçalves (who painted the famous San Vicente panels in the Museu Nacional de Arte Antiga in Lisbon) to produce a picture depicting the episode of the Pentecost from the New Testament for the altar of the same chapel. This painting, unfortunately no longer in existence, does lend credence to the idea that the fresco painting of the walls of the church may also have been ordered by Dom Afonso V.

Alfonso's successor – his son Dom João II (1455–95) – having fulfilled the official days of mourning following his father's death, was proclaimed king in the palace at Sintra. The public ceremony was held with great pomp in the Jogo da Pela – one of the building's many terraces and courtyards. And it was also this palace that was the scene, in 1492, of the decision of the same Dom João II to receive in Portugal (in exchange for the payment of a large sum of money) the Jews expelled from Spain by the Catholic kings – a decision of far-reaching political and social consequences.

But it is to Dom Manuel I, designated heir to the throne by Dom João II, that we owe the most profound and significant changes to the palace, comparable only to those carried out by Dom João I nearly 100 years earlier.

To begin with – and we know this from the building contract – Dom Manuel I devoted himself to improving and embellishing the existing building. From around 1497 to 1510 he remodelled almost all of the windows and doorways, lending them a grandeur and decoration characteristic of late Gothic artistic splendour. He embellished the interiors of the existing living rooms and bedchambers, lining the walls with compositions of *azulejos* (ceramic tiles) in a highly decorative style that made the most of the possibilities of illusion and the reverberation of light afforded by this ancient Islamic tradition. He rearranged the links between the various existing buildings with the creation of several courtyards that are responsible, along with the apparent disorganization of the whole complex, for the variety of perspectives and intimate spaces that give the palace at Sintra its exceptional character.

To complete this initial work by Dom Manuel I, the importance of water was reasserted and accentuated: fountains, ponds and water-spouts helped to ensure it took its place as an essential element of the *personality* of the palace. Its refreshing presence, the continuous sound of it flowing into ponds or the soft murmur of the gentle trickles falling into the marble vessel in the Sala dos Árabes (Arab Room), the reflection of the buildings mirrored in its smooth surface, duplicating

them and rendering their image fragile, its symbolic and ultimate evocation of *Life* and *Regeneration* – give water an important role in our understanding and experience of the palace. It is doubtless one of the elements that most clearly accentuates the way the Mudéjar style – the continuity of Islamic artistic traditions and sensibilities in the Iberian Peninsula throughout the Middle Ages – flourished in Portugal, particularly in the fifteenth and early sixteenth centuries.

Dom Manuel I's work on the palace at Sintra did not stop with these renovations, however. From 1510 onwards, he built an entirely new palace complex – the so-called Manueline Wing (today used largely for the services that run the historic building), which takes the form of another palace, itself complete and entirely independent of the existing one. In contrast with the decoration of the windows of the earlier palace, this new architectural complex uses carved elements of great sculptural force, according to the highly naturalistic decorative grammar characteristic of Manueline art.

Dom Manuel I was also responsible for the construction of another building that replaced the former Casa de Meca (House of Mecca) – a name that still, in the early sixteenth century, clearly referred back to the Arabic origins of the old palace of Sintra. At the highest point of the rocky hill on which the palace stands, he built, to replace the Casa de Meca, a quadrangular tower topped by a tall pyramid, which was completed around 1517–18. In its interior, a vast room – the Sala dos Brasões (Coat of Arms Room) – has an immense ceiling that is decorated in a unique way: in the centre of the ceiling is the king's coat of arms, surrounded by those of the other members of the royal family and, set further back, the heraldic shields of 72 noble families of the kingdom.

If other of Dom Manuel I's palaces exhibited a similar decoration (and we are not aware that they did), this would in no way lessen the impact and importance of the genuine *Book of Gold of the*

11. Aerial view of the
palace with the square
block of the Sala dos
Brasões standing on the
highest point of the rock

12. Decorative detail of
Manueline art in the
Gruta dos Banhos

13. Renaissance fireplace
in the Sala das Pegas

14. Detail of the ceramic
floor in the Quarto de
Dom Afonso VI

Nobility constituted by the ceiling decoration of the Sala dos Brasões through its heraldic and genealogical subject matter. As it is, this is the only decoration of its kind to have been preserved, and so it can be seen as a very powerful element that reflects the originality of the palace at Sintra not only in Portugal but also in Europe as a whole.

After the reign of Dom Manuel I, the various Portuguese monarchs that followed him, although concerned with the maintenance and habitability of the palace at Sintra, did not use it with such frequency. This is reflected in the fact that, between the sixteenth and seventeenth centuries, perhaps the most important function of the palace was that of a prison for an unfortunate dethroned king – Dom Afonso VI (1643–83) – who spent his last nine years living there in exile. Tradition has it that the rooms used by the king during this period were those that give access, through the Sala Chinesa (Chinese Room), to the upper gallery of the palace chapel. His bedchamber, known as the Quarto de Dom Afonso VI, still has its original medieval flooring which, in its similarity with that of the chancel of the palace, is also one of the oldest and most important remnants of the fifteenth-century palace.

The Lisbon earthquake of 1755, responsible for the violent destruction of the lower part of the city, was also felt strongly in Sintra and its palace. Contemporary reports of this disaster stress and

15. Sala das Galés: detail of the ceiling painting – a Turkish galleon

16. Glazed tile with vine-leaf and tendril design in relief (early sixteenth century): Sala de Dom Sebastião

17. *Sintra drawn from the south side* (Duarte de Armas, *Livro das Fortalezas*). Standing above the Sala dos Árabes, and displaying the large royal flag, is the tower that was completely destroyed by the earthquake. Coll. I.A.N./ Torre do Tombo

lament the ruinous state in which the palace was left. Among the most visible consequences was the loss of the great tower that had stood above the Sala dos Árabes and that appeared in the drawings (included in *Livro das Fortalezas*) that Duarte de Armas had made of the palace in 1509.

By 1781, the great restoration campaign of the building was already under way, particularly in the Sala dos Cisnes and in the Câmara das Pegas. If we look at the building contract for this work, under the supervision of the architect of the Casa Real and chief engineer José Manuel de Carvalho Negreiros, one detail of great significance stands out: there was, on the part of the restorers, a concern to respect the original plan of the building as much as possible, a fact that anticipates in a remarkable way the concern and respect for conserving our historic heritage that was a characteristic of the second half of the twentieth century. From the re-use of materials to the manufacture of ones similar to those that were lost, every effort was made to reduce to a minimum the destruction caused by the earthquake.

The work did involve new costs, however, particularly with regards to the *azulejos* lining the walls of the various rooms, which of course required a great deal of work. This explains why so many of these sets were recomposed or simply abandoned, why some tiles were re-used in areas where they were not necessarily to be found originally, and why yet others were salvaged from heaps found in forgotten stores.

A significant change was also made by the installation of Moorish-style battlements on top of the main façades of the Dom João Building and the Manueline Wing, based on the idea (which began to

take root in the second half of the eighteenth century) that the whole palace was a vestige of the ancient palace of the Muslim fortress.

The National Palace of Sintra breathed its last as a royal residence during the nineteenth century. However, before that time (from 1787 and following the reconstruction work to repair the damage caused by the 1755 earthquake), Dona Maria I (Dona Maria Pia, 1734–1816) had alterations carried out to the Manueline Wing, dividing rooms and chambers into the small rooms that were fashionable at the time. According to the testimony of the English traveller William Beckford, who was writing in the nineteenth century, these alterations in no way contributed to the dignity of the palace, as we can still see in the places where these changes have been retained. Even the ground-floor portico that served as support to the Sala dos Cisnes, and through which the visitor today enters the palace, was closed off in order to form another two or three rooms.

From 1838, the desire of Dom Fernando (Ferdinand of Saxe-Coburg Gotha), the husband of Dona Maria II (1819–53), to transform the ruined Pena Jeronymite Monastery into a palace, meant that the royal family stayed at Sintra more frequently. Although the old palace saw more occupants during this period, nothing notable in terms of art was added to it.

The last queen of Portugal, Dona Amelia de Orleãs e Bragança (1865–1951), did pay very special attention to this royal residence. In truth, and according to the testimony of the Conde de Sabugosa (transcribed in his book *O Paço de Sintra*), the queen, 'attracted by the indescribable spell cast by this palace on anyone who looks upon it, drew in her notebook one of the Manueline windows of the part of the palace that was her first lodging'. Other drawings were to follow, and if the value of these drawings is relative in strictly artistic terms, in historical terms they are of undeniable importance.

18. *Opposite* Gruta dos
Banhos in the Central
Courtyard: eighteenth-cen-
tury glazed tile decoration

19. *Above* Gruta dos
Banhos: detail of the decorative plasterwork on the
ceiling (second half of the
eighteenth century)

20. *Left* Sala dos Cisnes:
sixteenth-century *azulejos*
re-used and reset during
the second half of the
eighteenth century

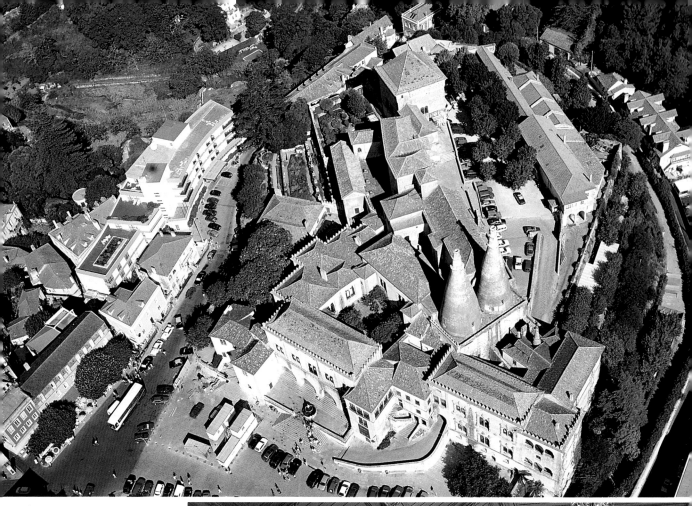

21. Aerial view of the palace, clearly showing the layout and organization of its buildings

22. Manueline Room, entirely refurbished in the mid-twentieth century by the architect Raúl Lino

23. Portico beneath the Sala dos Cisnes

It was specifically the anthology of these drawings that inspired the Conde de Sabugosa to write and publish, in 1903, the first monograph on the palace – *O Paço de Sintra* – an essential work even today (and in certain aspects irreplaceable) for an understanding of many of the historical incidents for which this building provided the stage or setting.

With the end of the monarchy and the proclamation of the republic in 1910, the palace was made state property and declared a national monument. Restoration and alteration work, directed by the architect Raúl Lino in the 1940s, attempted to restore the appearance that was considered original of a centuries-old palace. At the same time, this architect proceeded to decorate the palace with a whole set of works of art from former royal collections or acquired specifically for it, since practically none of the original furniture had been preserved.

The new role to be played by the National Palace of Sintra was that of museum. Its unique nature as the only remaining Portuguese medieval royal residence (as we have stressed from the beginning) makes it particularly well-suited to the task.

24. The magnificent
expanse of the landscape
surrounding the palace
(viewed from the top of
the Serra de Sintra), with
the Atlantic Ocean in the
background

RESIDENCES AND MEANINGS

Examining in detail the principal historic moments of its existence does not give the final word on the importance of the National Palace of Sintra. In parallel with the material existence of its walls and spaces, the reality of the palace was also built with an imaginative flare that, over the centuries, gradually lent it a diaphanous cloak in which legend and poetry joined hand in hand to create in it another reality.

The first time that the palace at Sintra was the explicit subject of a reflection on its virtues as the favoured residence of the monarchs of Portugal is found, as we have said, in the words of Dom Duarte. In a letter dated 24 July 1435, conferring privileges on the town of Sintra (see Conde de Sabugosa, *O Paço de Sintra*, 1903), the king lists the specific reasons why he favoured this palace as a summer residence: the excellent mountain air and water; the abundance of food from the land and sea; the proximity of Lisbon; the very existence, finally, of these 'noble palaces with very exten-sive views' is how he classes his residence in Sintra in that document. It is interesting to see how Sintra continues to attract visitors for the very same reasons.

One of the palace's attributes mentioned by the king arouses considerable astonishment for its modernity. His appreciation of the 'very extensive views' afforded by the palace – a reflection of the aesthetic attitude shown by a king who loved nature (and specifically the wild beauty of the Sintra landscape) and the sea that can be glimpsed from there – the contemplation of which, from the win-dows and verandas of those 'noble palaces', would undoubtedly bring him the consolation and peace of spirit that, at a particular period of his life, he had lost.

The passion felt by Dom Duarte for this royal residence led him almost to prophecy, in the intro-duction of his letter of 1435 mentioned above, that his successors would feel the same attraction: 'we came to this town of Sintra many times to spend the summer. And this we believed the Kings who came after us would do'. And, as if to confirm this aesthetic sense and the high opinion in which Sintra and its palace were held throughout the fifteenth century, we have the heart-felt cry of a foreigner – Nicolau Valckenstein – on leaving Portugal in 1451, accompanying Dom Duarte's daugh-ter for her marriage with the Emperor of Germany: '*O Sintra amaenissimus locus et hortus regius . . .*' ['Oh Sintra, most delightful place and royal garden . . .'].

In the sixteenth century, the royal historian and humanist Damião de Góis gives, in relation to the preference also shown by Dom Manuel I for the palace at Sintra, the same reasons already expressed by Dom Duarte. He shares the same delight in the airiness and cheerfulness of the palace in summer ('one of the freshest and most pleasant places in Europe, for any king, prince or lord to be able to spend his time there') and extols the quality of the waters ('the finest and coolest springs in the whole of Estremadura'), the abundance of game ('here there is much hunting of deer and other beasts') and the excellent fruit ('many fine fruits of all the kinds that can be found in all

25. The 'grandiose and magnificent palace of the kings of Portugal', as described by Damião de Góis in the second half of the sixteenth century

26. Sala de Dom Sebastião

27. Sala das Galés: detail of ceiling painting – a Portuguese galleon

Hispania'). Furthermore, when describing the city of Lisbon, the same Damião de Góis curiously included among its principal buildings the 'grandiose and magnificent palace of the kings of Portugal, which is called Sintra, taking its name from the Serra'.

Although Damião de Góis closely follows the virtues already stated by Dom Duarte in the above description of the palace, he adds a couple of new advantages of his own in relation to the Serra de Sintra and the royal building. He describes the mountain range as being 'one of the freshest and most pleasant places in Europe' and the palace as being responsible for the increase in importance and esteem of the mountain itself: 'the flavour of all these things is increased by the magnificent palaces which the kings have in this place'.

In the middle of the sixteenth century, this comparison made by Damião de Góis of Portugal with the other countries of Europe is one of the unexpected cultural aspects of the time. The importance of the palace at Sintra increases significantly as it becomes, in this context, a national symbol of the excellence of the Portuguese nation as a whole: 'most noble palaces, that in Hespanha there are none more beautiful', as the poet António Coelho Gasco described them (see Visconde de Juromenha, *Cintra Pinturesca*, 1838).

The final appraisal of Damião de Góis should be understood in the same way. The palace is 'magnificent' because, being the residence of the monarch and the place where royal power is exercised and displayed, it surpasses all the natural qualities of the Serra de Sintra. Indeed, 'it adds to its flavour'.

An interesting Latin poem composed by Luísa Sigea, lady-in-waiting to Princess Maria, daughter of Dom Manuel I (see Conde de Sabugosa, *O Paço de Sintra*, 1903), thus takes on additional significance. The poem is on the theme of the prophecy of a nymph who promises the aforementioned princess the imperial throne. Luísa Sigea uses as an introduction the description of Sintra and its bucolic charms, in which the royal palace is included in its own right.

28. Nature still succeeds
in contributing its
vigorous beauty to the
attraction of the National
Palace of Sintra today

29. Sala dos Cisnes: the
main hall of the palace is
its largest and most
distinctive space. Swans
adorn the ceiling panels

In the sixteenth century, the Serra de Sintra is the subject of a major re-evaluation on the part of the humanists, in the context of a pagan and mythological vision taken from classical antiquity: the Sacred Mountain or the Promontory of the Moon as the Latin writers had baptized it, now becomes a pagan Olympus or a newly rediscovered Eden. Damião de Góis, himself a humanist, does not hesitate in echoing legendary traditions that assert that the quality of the soil of the region of Sintra is such that 'mares conceive without external intervention' or that in the nearby sea at Colares, in a cave beaten by the ocean, 'our people believe that a Triton was once seen there singing with its shell'. In this context of the sanctification of the whole of the nature of Sintra, the palace is, finally, one of the specific and material elements that best define and sustain this humanist vision: 'a garden of earthly paradise / That Solomon sent here / For a king of Portugal' – as the poet and dramatist Gil Vicente (c.1465–c.1537) was to define it. The mythification of Sintra and its palace, although in a different context, was to be taken to its furthest consequences in the

30. *Right* Sala dos Cisnes: sixteenth-century tiles have been reused to create this eighteenth-century fantastical design of military architecture in sgraffito

31. *Below* Sala da Audiência: it is here that, according to tradition, Dom Sebastião listened to the poet Luís de Camões read *The Lusiads*

nineteenth century. In fact, the Romantic movement valued, among other means of declaring itself, the quest for exoticism and a fascination with an Orient replete with the mysteries of *The Arabian Nights*. In the Iberian Peninsula a building already existed with all these particular qualities and which therefore soon became a place of pilgrimage to artists, writers and scholars: the Alhambra Palace in Granada.

In this context, the rediscovery and reappraisal of the peninsula's Moorish past and admiration for the masterpiece represented by the palace at Granada, began to influence the vision of writers and artists both at home and abroad (Lord Byron being one of the most notable) who, when they came to Sintra, tried very hard to find in the town's medieval palace, a duplicate of that other Arab palace in Granada.

32. Detail of the palace that appears to confirm the view of Charles Frédéric Merveilleux (1738): 'built without order and in fragments'

Significantly, perhaps the first reference to the detection of Moorish style in the palace at Sintra was made by a foreigner, Charles Frédéric Merveilleux, in a book published in Amsterdam in 1738 (*Mémoires instructifs pour un voyageur dans les divers États de L'Europe*), and earlier, therefore, than the influence of the Romantic movement. 'The Serra de Sintra dominates the Town and the Castle or Royal Palace, built without order and in fragments, since the Christians became the masters of Portugal. It is in Moorish style, with no fine gardens or any of the attractions essential to a Royal House'.

Although this evaluation is, in general, a negative one (according to the mental and aesthetic predisposition of Charles Merveilleux), exactly 100 years after its publication, A. D. de Castro e Souza took up and expanded this idea in what will have also been, in effect, the first description of the palace at Sintra. In contrast with the negative evaluation of Charles Merveilleux, however, Castro e Souza's appraisal of the building was entirely positive: 'a masterpiece in the Order of Arab, or rather Moorish, Architecture. At each step the elegance, grace, fantasy and delicacy of the ancient oriental chisel excel. Sublime and majestic architecture, colossal, without monotony and moderation, but rich with variety; not silent and mute, but animated and lively, making the stones speak'.

The most significant aspect of this interpretation lies in the names used by A. D. de Castro e Souza for certain areas of the palace, typically Arabic names not encountered before in any other writer, such as the Jardim de Lindaraia and the Sala das Duas Irmãs (Room of the Two Sisters; interestingly a room in the Alhambra of Granada has the exact same name).

The Moorish origins and the Arab names attributed to parts of the palace at Sintra, after the description by A. D. de Castro e Souza, then take on the force of an accepted truth to the extent that, in 1842, four years after the publication of his book, another foreign traveller, Prince Felix Lichnowsky, goes even further and views the Arabic origins of the palace as a definite fact borne out by these very names: 'It seems unquestionable that this residence was formerly the Alhambra of the Moorish kings in Lisbon, as is shown by the Arabic architecture of some parts, particularly the chimneys, the fountains and the running water distributed around the whole building, and more particularly the Arab names still used for some of the palace's rooms'.

The hasty confusion conveyed by these appraisals, resulted in the conviction that the palace at Sintra was not only of Arabic origin (which in fact turned out to be correct) but also that the existing building was, in many of its spaces and construction materials, the authentic Moorish building put up between the remote tenth and twelfth centuries (which turns out to be very difficult to sustain historically): 'People who have visited the Alhambra in Granada and the Palace of Sintra' wrote Inácio Vilhena Barbosa in 1864, 'must have noted various points of similarity that exist between the two buildings'.

That this was the prevailing view is confirmed by the caution with which, in spite of everything, a foreigner – Albrecht Haupt – refers to this subject in the early twentieth century. After noting that the Portuguese considered the palace at Sintra as the Portuguese Alhambra, he is at pains to add: 'Not that one wishes with this to assert that the palace that we see today could have belonged, even in part, to the period of Arab domination'.

Reminders of the former palace of the Moorish fortress are indeed very much alive in the National Palace of Sintra. They do not, however, lie in any physical survival of the Moorish building, but rather in the adoption of a Mudéjar style that, as an integral aspect of the art of the Iberian

36. Sala dos Brasões: glazed tile composition on the wall depicting a chivalric scene (eighteenth century)

37. Detail of the lacework on the ceiling of the palace chapel

38. Detail of one of the swans painted on the ceiling of the room that takes its name from the birds – the Sala dos Cisnes

Peninsula throughout the early Middle Ages, is manifested in the palace at Sintra in the intimacy of its many courtyards and varied gardens, in the lining of its walls with highly decorative compositions of *azulejos*, in the chapel ceiling where the *alfarge* or lacework rekindled the Arab memory of its earliest owners, and, above all, in the ubiquitous presence of water throughout the palace.

In any case, and after the mythical re-creations of Romanticism, the historical and architectural truths of National Palace of Sintra can no longer be summed up with any certainty. The legends of the Sala das Pegas (Magpie Room) and the Sala dos Cisnes (Swan Room), created by someone for the building, give it an aura of timelessness that can only be the product of the imagination; the new names that were attributed to some of its spaces in the modern period – Jardim de Lindaraia, Sala das Duas Irmãos, Sala dos Árabes – if they were indeed taken (directly or by mere suggestion) from the Alhambra in Granada, add a complicit exoticism to this other palace set high in the magical Serra.

39. Sculptural group on
the fountain in the centre
of the Sala dos Árabes

40. Central Courtyard
viewed from the Gruta dos
Banhos

It is from this mountain that one really gleans a definitive understanding of the palace at Sintra.
It is to one of the pioneering creations of European Romanticism – the Pena Palace, standing on top
of the Serra de Sintra – that one should perhaps look for a final understanding of the National Palace
of Sintra itself. Built by Dom Fernando II (1816–85) on the site of a ruined Jeronymite monastery, it
was done in a language that intentionally recreated the grammar and defining features of
Manueline art, a concept that was being invented in Portugal at that precise moment.

Crowning one of the highest and steepest summits of the Serra and taking on the role of a
Romantic and complicit duplication of the medieval palace that stood at its feet, Pena Palace, crys-
tallized all the dreams, all the imagination, all the sacralization and demiurgic power of a mountain,
which the national palace of the town resembled and with which it definitively blended.

41. Aerial view of the
palace, showing in the
foreground the extensive
Dona Amélia Terrace,
formerly the main
entrance courtyard

EXTERIOR

DONA AMÉLIA TERRACE

We enter the National Palace of Sintra through the Dona Amélia Terrace. This name pays homage to the last queen of Portugal, who devoted particular attention to this residence. We should not forget, however, that the space it designates was the former walled courtyard that stood, as in all medieval palaces, in front of the royal quarters.

In the case of the palace at Sintra, this main courtyard was confined on its south and east sides by rows of compact buildings used to accommodate nobles and their retinues when visiting the king, as well as the officials and household staff of the palace.

A plan dated 1902, published by the Conde de Sabugosa in *O Paço de Cintra*, still shows the location and internal organization of these buildings, which – despite the probable modesty of their construction – added to the group's sense of monumentality and helped to define more clearly the true dimensions of a royal palace. Furthermore, they had already been depicted in the drawings of the palace made by Duarte de Armas in the first decade of the sixteenth century – clear evidence of their antiquity and the importance of their functions. Unfortunately, this entire group of buildings was demolished after 1910, the year Portugal was proclaimed a republic. So we have lost not only an understanding of the living quarters and service structures that complemented the core royal residence, but also a sense of the seclusion and privacy enjoyed by the palace, like all the other similar medieval buildings, by not being exposed to the outside in such a visible way.

The sense of intimacy that used to characterize the terrace (and which further amplified the surprising effect caused by the monumental chimneys), has given way to a degree of exposure. Although this has opened up the view for the visitor, it has destroyed one of the most defining features of the palace complex – the protected and defended aspect of its image and therefore also of its occupants and owners. It is, in a way, the retention of a medieval sense of defence, an evocation of the historical times when the warlike fortification was transformed into a palace, that has been lost completely.

The elevated platform on which the Dona Amélia Terrace stands draws attention to the stark differences in height between the various buildings of the palace. This close adaptation of the building to its elevated site is one of the factors directly responsible for the apparently complicated and confused organization that, while it lends the palace much of the picturesqueness and originality praised by nineteenth-century writers, can provoke in the mind of the first-time visitor a sensation of total incomprehension of the sense and layout of the spaces.

According to the Conde de Sabugosa, this main courtyard was used in former times for bull-running, jousting and the holding of tournaments. It was chosen because it was the largest of all the palace's courtyards; it was also the one nearest the perimeter and so could be accessed by an outside audience without affecting the privacy of the palace.

MAIN FAÇADE

The main façade of the palace, overlooking the Dona Amélia Terrace and oriented perceptibly toward the east, has to be read as a function of its two basic structures: the first, built in the reign of Dom João I, corresponds to the Sala dos Cisnes and is framed by two small salient tower-like structures; the second, to the visitor's right, is the wing built by Dom Manuel during the second decade of the sixteenth century.

Joining these two structures is another intermediate one, smaller and less important, which was erected later in the sixteenth century to facilitate communication between the two buildings. This was achieved by building on the terraces that preceded both the Sala dos Cisnes and the state room of the Manueline Wing.

In this intermediate structure, in the area closest to the Sala dos Cisnes, is a discreet external staircase standing against the wall, which has existed at least since the sixteenth century. In the early twentieth century – and once more according to the testimony of the Conde de Sabugosa – this staircase was still the main access to the buildings of the palace at Sintra.

DOM JOÃO BUILDING

The part of the main façade built by Dom João I, rectangular in plan, is protected at either end by two projecting structures that are reminiscent of small watchtowers. The one on the left was changed the most following the 1755 Lisbon earthquake. It has on its ground floor a delicate marble door, decorated with Renaissance carvings, which was probably taken from another part of this or even an entirely different royal palace. Until the sixteenth century, the tower on the right ended in a terrace covered with a roof standing on supports, but it was then closed in and turned into the Sala dos Archeiros (Halberdiers' Room).

The main part of this façade, with its long access staircase from the courtyard and circular fountain on the intermediate landing, is divided into two floors. The ground floor consists of a portico, defined by four austere, wide, pointed arches. Originally, these did not give direct access to the palace interior. The numerous stonemason's marks on each of the arches suggest a rapid and very precise campaign.

As well as being an essential element of support for the room on the floor above, this portico – which the documentation of the period refers to as a *lógea* or loggia – is evidence of the survival of a curious structure that developed throughout the Middle Ages and was related to the execution of public deeds and the manifestation of the power of the master of the palace.

The creation of some windows in the interior walls of this portico of the main façade of the palace at Sintra gave the occupants a view of the events – such as ceremonies and festivities – taking place in the main courtyard below. Only in 1721, according to the date inscribed on one of the steps, was the staircase built that today gives us access to the palace interior. And the vault that covers this portico was the result of restoration work following the great Lisbon earthquake of 1755.

The upper floor of the façade is defined by five rectangular windows, organized symmetrically around the central one. In order to fulfil its pivotal function, this is more elaborate and formed into a balcony window with twisted columns, in contrast to the plain shafts of the central columns of the other windows. Originally, these windows are likely to have been simpler. The present limestone twin arches, decorated with borders on their intrados, as well as the fine columns and their respective bases and capitals of white marble, are the result of the improvements carried out by Dom Manuel I in the early sixteenth century, and will have lent additional grandeur to this group built by Dom João I. The marbles correspond to pieces imported from Genoa throughout the sixteenth century. In addition to those in the National Palace of Sintra, many similar capitals still exist today scattered about the country, especially in the Estremadura and Alentejo regions.

The slightly flamboyant twin arches of the windows of the Sala dos Cisnes fit inside a rectangle that defines the characteristic *alfiz* of Arabic tradition and that once more confirms the intervention of Dom Manuel I, in whose reign the Mudéjar style saw a remarkable renaissance and spread.

44. Ground-floor portico beneath the Sala dos Cisnes, giving a glimpse of the Old Town of Sintra and the mountains

45. The main façade of the palace, showing the Sala dos Cisnes in the Dom João building

46. Main façade of the
Manueline Wing of the
palace

MANUELINE BUILDING

The Manueline Wing was designed as an extension to the Dom João
Building, thereby increasing the size of the main façade and with it the
image of grandeur of the whole palace. For this reason, and because of
the steep gradients of the site, the new wing is built to match, on the
same level, the noble storey of the Sala dos Cisnes. It is also worth
pointing out the L-shaped design of the whole of this wing of the palace,
an unusual feature for the period in which it was built.

As well as this original aspect, it is curious to note how the design of
the stately façade of the Manueline Building is organized into two
entirely separate sections, which give us an understanding, from the
outside, of the difference in internal organization. In fact, while the
largest wall is split, on each of the two upper floors, into three highly-
decorated double windows (with the central ones taking a pivotal role
as before), suggesting rooms used for grander functions (in this case,
the state room), the building at the end is not only slightly lower but also
opens into two delicate verandas with three simple arches, suggesting
its link to more restricted and intimate areas of the palace: the
antechamber, the bedchamber and the inner room. This is in fact a true
hallmark of medieval buildings; a clear indication of their internal
organization from the outside.

The windows of the noble Manueline Building are fine examples of
the essential characteristics of the art of the reign of Dom Manuel I. In
fact, the architectural structures that frame the window-openings are
transformed into intertwining tree-trunks with their truncated branches
in an intensely naturalistic design topped with ripe pomegranates or
bulbous artichokes, repeated on a smaller scale on the intrados of the
windows, thereby replacing the borders. We should not, however, be
distracted by this extreme naturalism from seeing the precise symbolism
that is integral to it: whether fruits or tree-trunks, they are specific signs of
a heraldic and genealogical language that, in the reign of Dom Manuel I,
was a manifestation of one of the main preoccupations of the monarch,
the reorganization of society and the reinforcement of the absolute
state. Furthermore, these concerns and the heraldic language used in
the decorative sculpture of the windows were to be given one of their

most transcendental manifestations in the extraordinary heraldic decoration of the ceiling of the Sala dos Brasões (Coat of Arms Room), the last area to be built by the aforementioned Dom Manuel I.

In contrast with the rich decoration of the two noble floors of this wing, the ground floor – defined by simple doors with round arches and small quadrangular windows – is reminiscent, in its plain sturdiness, of the entrance to a fortress, thus amplifying the aesthetic and truly scenographic effect of the grand windows above.

Both the Dom João Building and the Manueline Wing are crowned by Moorish-style pyramid capped brick merlons, which, to the visitor's eye, give a clear impression of the palace's Arab past. But these are in fact the result of restoration work carried out after the 1755 earthquake, giving form to the idea (that was beginning to take hold at that time) that the palace at Sintra was the Portuguese rival of the Alhambra of Granada. In fact, the convincing and specific evidence of the drawings made by Duarte de Armas in the early sixteenth century show the building indeed crowned with battlements, but of the type that were used commonly at that time throughout the country, on both civil and religious buildings. In other words, the kind known as bevelled battlements, which had no military function and were purely decorative. This type of battlement signified only the noble social condition of the owners, and was, once again, a specifically heraldic feature.

47. Window detail of the Manueline Wing, showing lopped tree branches and pomegranates carved in a naturalistic style

48. Window detail of the Manueline Wing, showing artichokes among its decorative elements

49. The central window of the Sala Manuelina

50. North façade of the palace: the entrance to the chapel is off a small terrace

51. The top line of buildings make up the north wing and include the kitchens, chapel and Sala dos Brasões

NORTH FAÇADE

Going up a ramp on the right-hand side of the main Dom João Building that passes beneath the intermediate building joining the Dom João and Manueline Wing, the visitor enters a long terrace known as the Jogo da Pela (Ball Game).

A long narrow pavilion on the right, which formerly housed the palace stables, was extended and improved in the early years of the sixteenth century on the orders of Dom Manuel I. On the left, following one another at successively higher levels, are the fifteenth-century kitchens (with the immense chimneys assuming their most imposing dimensions on this side of the palace); the chapel, on an upper landing and with the small terrace along the side façade serving as a churchyard; and, at an even higher level and reached by an external flight of stairs, the rectangular block of the oldest part of the palace. The sequence of buildings is completed, finally, by the quadrangular building of the sixteenth-century Sala dos Brasões, unusually dramatic in its form, location and dimensions.

This is the most distant and hidden façade of the palace, and it is also, perhaps as a consequence, the simplest and most austere. From its location, and according to records dating from the end of the Middle Ages, it is likely to have been the part used by the queens of Portugal when they were staying in Sintra.

It is interesting to note that, following the 1755 earthquake, efforts were made to recreate the appearance – in terms of number, location and design – of the window-openings. This can easily be seen if we compare this part of the building with the drawing of it made by Duarte de Armas at the end of the first decade of the sixteenth century. Although almost all the windows were rebuilt after the earthquake, they are in the same place and (almost all) the contours of the window-openings are as they were redesigned in the time of Dom Manuel I.

In addition to the chapel door on this side of the palace, which allowed servants and residents to enter to attend liturgical services, there is another door that gives access to the interior of the palace buildings situated at the top of the external flight of stairs already mentioned. Located in the small building that stands proud, in the form of a tower, indicating the axis of this palace building, this is an entrance that lends itself naturally to the separate and independent use of the various buildings that make up the National Palace of Sintra.

52. Sintra drawn from the east-southeast (Duarte de Armas, *Livro das Fortalezas*) Coll. I.A.N. / Torre do Tombo

53. North façade of the palace, on the level of the palace chapel (visible in the foreground on the left): in the background, the Sala dos Brasões

54. The royal coat of arms and those of the princes, sons of Dom Manuel I, in the centre of the ceiling of the Sala dos Brasões

SALA DOS BRASÕES

The Sala dos Brasões (Coat of Arms Room), the final building that makes up the north façade, is, from the outside, an immense cube with a practically square plan that is oriented precisely according to the cardinal points. The double windows that open on its four sides, indicating the noble floor, serve to break the monotony of this building's lack of adornment. The only exception to this sobriety – the only showiness, as the Conde de Sabugosa described it – lies in the delicate band of decoration at the top of the walls beneath the roof, offering its many orifices as shelter to pigeons.

This external bareness, this compact mass built on the highest point of the hill, might spark off an intriguing doubt in the mind of the visitor, who will perhaps wonder what awaits him or her in the interior of this imposing and well-defended building.

The Sala dos Brasões is extended at the back by walls resembling a bulwark of modern fortification, which contain within them the so-called Pátio dos Tanquinhos. There are two broad windows in these walls: the one facing north depicts two armillary spheres, the personal emblem of Dom Manuel I. This is the only place on either of the external faces of the palace where this identifying symbol of the king, sculpted in stone, is offered to the eyes of the visitor.

55. Aerial view of the
palace, showing the
gardens to the south,
laid out in terraces

56. Detail of the Jardim
de Lindaraia or Jardim
do Principe, with the
Sala dos Brasões
visible on the left

GARDENS

Outside the palace the visitor can explore (or at least take a look at) the various gardens that are an integral part of the personality of the National Palace of Sintra.

They are all located, as we might expect, on the southern slope of the hill, both because of its gentler gradient and because it catches the most sun. Arranged like this, the various gardens accentuate the progressive rise of the side façades of the various buildings that, on this side, occupy successively higher levels of the hillside on which the whole palace is built.

The southern slope provides the best observation point (somewhat hampered by several trees) of the seemingly disordered complexity of the buildings that make up the National Palace of Sintra: the progression in height of the various buildings; their location in always unexpected perspectives; the variety of the shape and location of the windows; the diversity and autonomy of the roofs; the suggested spaces of the gardens and secret places that add to this diversity and form the most varied and, admittedly, picturesque and spectacular side of the National Palace of Sintra.

In the second half of the sixteenth century, on his visit to Portugal (whose crown he had also taken possession of), the King Felipe II of Spain (1527–98) was so impressed by these gardens that he did not stint in his admiration and praise for them in his correspondence with his daughters: '*tiene jardines y fuentes . . . y son buenos y muchos e muy buenas fuentes*' ('it has gardens and fountains . . . and they are fine and numerous [gardens] and very fine fountains').

The first and lowest garden encountered by the visitor is the Jardim da Preta (Garden of the Black Woman). It takes its name from a relief on a fountain that depicts, in a naïve composition, a black woman accompanied by a man in a red coat. A twisted column with decoration typical of the Manueline period, which used to stand in front of the palace, was relocated to this garden in the twentieth century.

Two further gardens – the Horta do Cipriano (Kitchen-garden of Cipriano) and the Jardim Novo (New Garden) follow the Jardim da Preta on a level with the 1902 building. Set on separate platforms,

57. The palace gardens,
arranged in terraces to
overcome the steep
gradient of the site

58. Sintra drawn from
the east side (Duarte de
Armas, *Livro das
Fortalezas*). The *'curral dos
coelhos'* or rabbit pen can
be seen on the left. Coll.
I.A.N. / Torre do Tombo

together with the Jardim da Preta, they occupy the site of the former *'curral dos coelhos'* or rabbit pen that Dom Manuel I ordered to be transformed in the early sixteenth century.

The last garden, further up, is the Jardim de Lindaraia or Jardim do Príncipe (Prince's Garden). In the drawing by Duarte de Armas, dated 1509, this area was an internal courtyard serving the so-called Casa de Meca. After the construction (in the sixteenth century?) of the independent building called the Sala das Galés, this garden then came to be lined, in practice, to that building.

Finally there is a striking courtyard known today as the Pátio da Estufa (Greenhouse Courtyard), which may have been designed as a veranda overlooking the old orchard. Small in area and today totally enclosed by buildings, this courtyard, which may have been deeper originally, occupies the base of the furthest building of the palace, and seems to correspond, according to the drawing by Duarte de Armas, to the Pomar da Rainha (Queen's Orchard), at that time a more open area. In 1510 Dom Manuel I ordered twenty-eight orange trees, forty-one peach trees, fourteen citron trees and three pear trees to be planted here.

INTERIOR

The entrance to the interior of the palace buildings is today via a flight of stone steps, which lack grandeur or monumentality, situated on the inside of the portico of Gothic arches beneath the Sala dos Cisnes. Built in the eighteenth century, they in no way correspond to the entrance of the medieval palace.

Once inside the building, the visitor must climb an elegant wide spiral staircase ascribed to the mid-sixteenth century – during the reign of Dom João III (1502–57) – and this is certainly consistent with its design. This takes us to a large vestibule that serves as a centre of access to the various buildings of the palace: opposite the visitor is the entrance to the monumental kitchen; to the right, the entrance to the Manueline Wing; and to the left, the door of the Sala dos Cisnes.

This vestibule is the result of uniting three different spaces: the terrace in front of the entrance to the Sala dos Cisnes, which Dom Duarte refers to in his description of the Palace of Sintra (see *O Livro dos Conselhos de el-rei D. Duarte*) as 'the terrace in front of the great hall' and which was later renamed the Sala dos Archeiros (Halberdiers' Room); an identical terrace in front of the Sala Manuelina; and the veranda that was then used to join them. The format of the original spaces can still be seen in the austere stone pillars that precisely mark out the terraces that preceded each of these rooms.

This reunification of spaces, probably carried out in the second half of the sixteenth century, was emphasized further when the walls were lined with *azulejos* of varied forms and colours that probably came from other areas of the palace. These immediately draw the visitor's attention to one of the most significant and original decorative riches of the palace at Sintra, in Portuguese and European terms: the enormous variety of glazed tile compositions. These *azulejos* line the walls of almost every room and building of the palace and, from hereon in, their bright and cheerful presence will be the visitor's constant companion. In fact, he or she can gaze upon examples of both Hispano-Arabic *corda seca* (a process of tile-making) and geometric tiles, and tiles with highly naturalistic vine leaves in relief (some of them combining the vine leaf with the tendril, others the vine leaf with the bunch of grapes). The predominance of blue tones on the geometric tiles and the emphasis on green in the naturalistic ones results in a chromatic palette of cold tones that creates an atmosphere of peaceful and refreshing luminosity.

Furthermore, the small fountain set into the wall, collecting its water in a delicate basin, not only amplifies this sensation of freshness but also immediately introduces the visitor to another of the characteristic features that give the interior of this palace its particular personality: the presence of clear and refreshing water, the constant (sometimes merely hinted) murmur and melody of which helps us to understand and to a certain extent to overcome some of the harshness of the ascending rhythm imposed by the various heights on which the different parts of the palace are built.

60. Fountain in the
palace vestibule

61. Sala dos Archeiros
(in the foreground),
showing the vestibule
that gives access to
the various palace
buildings

SALA MANUELINA

Before entering the set of buildings constructed by Dom João I, the visitor can see to his or her right the Sala Manuelina. The grand state room *par excellence*, this has been completely restored today, following the work carried out in the 1940s by the architect Raúl Lino. The *azulejos* were all produced at that time, in imitation of the sixteenth-century originals. The fireplace, recovered from another building, was restored and completed. The ceiling was designed and built in the same period. Only the doorways and windows are original, a notable example being the door in the wall at the far end, outlined with large mouldings in the form of ropes that support heavy fruits at the top. On the door-jamb to the right, a carefully drawn Y draws our attention to the architect who was probably responsible for building all the Manueline part of the palace: João Rodrigues, put in charge of the Sintra palaces in 1490 – still in the reign of Dom João II – and only replaced, due to illness and advanced age, only in 1526.

SALA DOS CISNES

62. Sala Manuelina, entirely restored (apart from the doors and windows) in the mid-twentieth century

63. Veranda of the Manueline Wing, serving as a passageway between the hall and the antechamber

64. Detail of the interior doorway of the Sala Manuelina, showing the mark of the six-teenth-century stone-mason who created it

Having looked at the main room of the Manueline Building, the visitor enters the first living space of the section erected by Dom João I in the early decades of the fifteenth century: the Sala dos Cisnes. Its considerable size (it is approximately 187m²), which is not so noticeable from the outside, makes it the largest room in the National Palace of Sintra.

In the residences of the kings and nobility of the Middle Ages, the *sala* was the largest and most external room, into which everyone, national or foreigner (except those being pursued by the law), might enter. This is where receptions, feasts, banquets and major ceremonies were held, making this room, as the most representative space of a medieval palace, an image of the building as a whole. Into it might enter, according to the words of Dom Duarte (see *Leal Conselheiro*), '*todollos do seu senhorio que omyzyados nom som e assy os estrangeiros que a ella querem vir*' (all those who are not pursued by justice including foreigners who wish to enter).

In the case of the Sala dos Cisnes, there is even some evidence that the inhabitants of Sintra were authorized to use it – from the times of Dom João II at the end of the fifteenth century – to hold their Holy Spirit festivals, which had been introduced, according to tradition, by Queen Santa Isabel (1269–1336) in the fourteenth century.

In fact, such highly exalted functions continue to this day in the Sala dos Cisnes of the National Palace of Sintra, as the Prime Minister of the Portuguese government frequently holds ceremonial receptions here for his foreign counterparts when they visit the country.

We enter the Sala dos Cisnes through a wide, white marble door, which, in its grandeur and the contour of its elements, clearly reveals the hand of Dom Manuel I, who had resolved to enhance the construction of his predecessor Dom João I in this way. Forming a rectangle with a slightly arched lintel, its structure consists of three small columns that go round the entire opening and are hardly interrupted by the minuscule capitals. Curiously, not only is the inner column the most elaborate

but it is also decorated with a twist that acts as an invitation to enter.

The Sala dos Cisnes was originally called simply the Sala Grande or Great Hall. During the reign of Dom Manuel I it was known as the Sala dos Infantes (Hall of the Princes). It owes its present name to the subject painted repeatedly on the twenty-seven wooden panels, separated by gilded pine cones inscribed in squares, that make up the ceiling – elegant white swans with gilded collars set in a naturalistic background – which must have been painted in the second half of the sixteenth century or in the seventeenth century. This whole ceiling had to be completely restored following the 1755 earthquake. The visual effect achieved by the rigid organization and systematic repetition of the swans in each of

65. Sala dos Cisnes

66. Entrance doorway to the Sala dos Cisnes

the octagons is, nevertheless, evocative, and breaks the monotony that might have resulted from the room's extensive area.

The openings into this room (two doors and eight large windows reaching right down to the floor) make a distinctive contribution to its sense of grandeur, with their outline in green (copper) and white (tin) *azulejos* arranged in a chequerboard pattern, and lining the walls up to mid-height. Although the majority of these *azulejos* date from the fifteenth and sixteenth centuries (except for those on the south wall, which are imitations put up in the twentieth century), they were restored following the damage wrought by the earthquake of 1755.

67. Fantastical military architecture in sgraffito made from glazed tiles in the eighteenth century (Sala dos Cisnes)

68. Mullion of the central window of the Sala dos Cisnes

69. Shield of the royal coat of arms in sgraffito made from glazed tiles (eighteenth century, Sala dos Cisnes)

The walls, windows and doors giving access to the Sala da Audiência are crowned with cut-out *azulejos* depicting Arab battlements, various fortresses and, over the south door, the royal coat of arms. Although all these *azulejos* are re-used, the sgraffito work (particularly of the royal coat of arms) calls our attention to the survival of techniques and the revival of neo-Moorish tastes in the middle of the eighteenth century. The *azulejos* take up the theme of the Moorish brick merlons on the outside of the building, which, as we have already seen, were added at the same time and were a clear expression of the same taste.

A large but plain white marble fireplace at the end of the Sala dos Cisnes reveals itself, by its columns and moulding, to be from the period of Dom Manuel I. Its installation is indicative of the desire for comfortable residences being felt by the nobility at the end of the Middle Ages.

A room of great splendour, the Sala dos Cisnes reflects – in its dimensions (intentional from the outset), in the later decorative work of the Manueline period and even in the post-earthquake restoration – not only the importance of this room in the structuring of the medieval palace, but also, in absolute terms, the primary place it occupies within the set of buildings that make up the National Palace of Sintra.

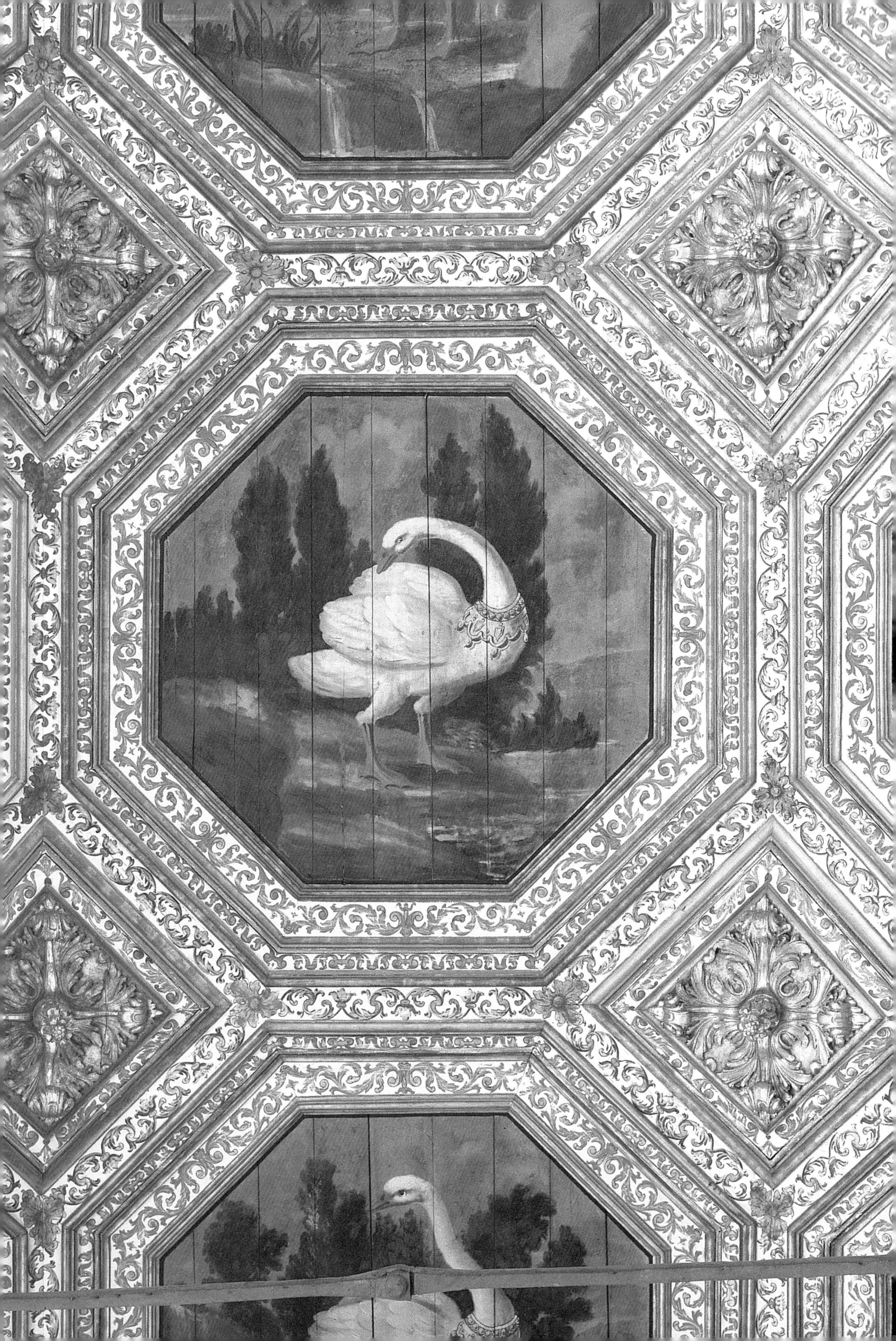

SALA DA AUDIÊNCIA

The door at the back of the Sala dos Cisnes leads to the so-called Sala da Audiência (Assembly Room) or Sala do Conselho (Council Room). Set in a small terrace not normally open to visitors, it is worth describing to the reader.

On one side of the terrace, a small covered area, in a Renaissance style visible in the columns and the architrave supporting the roof, houses a stone throne and a bench running round the wall; both are lined with Hispano-Arabic *azulejos*. Although these tiles date from the late fifteenth and early sixteenth centuries, they come from other parts of the palace (as do other sets that line the walls and benches of this area) following the principle of reusing materials that is a characteristic of this building.

A popular tradition holds that the Sala da Audiência was the place where the poet Luis de Camões read *The Lusiads* to Dom Sebastião (1554–78) or was at least where this monarch gave his final audience before leaving for the disastrous adventure of Alcácer-Quibir. Although these may be nothing more than well-meaning inventions, the name of this small terrace may perhaps correspond to its actual use, as it would have been in this area (formerly directly accessible to the exterior) that kings, when they were present at Sintra, would have received their subjects in audience or would have met with their officials for normal business.

The small open-air area underwent a great deal of restoration work in the twentieth century, although at the beginning of that century the courtyard was not only completely roofed but also had a door that communicated directly with the Sala das Pegas.

Returning to the Sala dos Cisnes, we go out through the small door at the side of the discreet fireplace onto a covered landing and continue the tour to the Pátio Central. Before doing this, we can see the way in which the Sala dos Cisnes stands entirely separate from the other buildings, since it is only this exterior passage that gives the visitor access to the room that follows. This fact accentuates, once again, the inherent functions of this public part of the palace, where everyone could enter, but from which only a very small number of people might have access to the privacy of the remaining rooms. Going down the stairs at the end of the porch, on the way out of the Sala dos Cisnes, we come to the Pátio Central or Pátio do Esguicho (Central Courtyard or Fountain Courtyard).

72. Central Courtyard, with
the powerful image of the
imposing kitchen chimneys

PÁTIO CENTRAL

This open-air space is central to the structure of all the palace buildings ordered to be built by Dom João I. Behind us is the Sala dos Cisnes; to the right, the kitchen; to the left, a set of chambers (including das Pegas, das Sereias and de Dom Sebastião); in front, the Sala dos Árabes and the Quarto de Hóspedes – in short, all the essential elements that make up a medieval palace and whose precise functions, with regards to the palace at Sintra, are known from the description given by Dom Duarte in the early fifteenth century. Two gigantic chimneys dominate the courtyard, like sentinels constantly on watch over all that surrounds them. Finally, the architectural importance of this courtyard is confirmed by the presence of grand balcony-windows on all of the buildings around it, of a kind not found on this scale in any other part of the royal residence.

On top of its structural function, the Pátio Central is further evidence to the visitor of the important role played by water in the National Palace of Sintra, not just as a decorative feature but also in defining its architectural personality and its life. From its presence in the shallow reservoir below the windows of the Sala dos Cisnes (which duplicates their image like a smooth mirror), through the central fountain springing from a Manueline twisted column (which is reminiscent of the pillories of the same period, and has on it the royal coat of arms held up by *putti* to remind us of the elevated lineage of the owners of the palace) to the Gruta (or Sala) dos Banhos (Bath House), it is water that, in its crystalline freshness and in its gentle and sensual murmuring on a calm afternoon, gives all the more originality to this open space in the interior of the palace.

Nevertheless, the Gruta dos Banhos, located at one end of the courtyard, is a building that is irresistibly reminiscent, if any doubt were to remain, of an Arab palace. The moulding on the three entrance arches and on the large embrasure that opens into the room at the far end, dates, without doubt, from the Manueline period. The figurative tiles that line the walls (with scenes in which water is the most conspicuous theme) and the polychrome plaster ceilings are, however, eighteenth- and nineteenth-century additions.

But the most surprising and original aspect of this space is the way in which water, emerging from small and almost invisible holes in the walls (and formerly also in the ceiling), not only cools the atmosphere but also takes the unwary visitor by surprise.

The structural function of this courtyard is completed by a set of passages that give direct access to the various buildings. On the side of the Gruta dos Banhos a small rectangular building houses a beautifully constructed spiral staircase attributable to the period of Dom João III, which links it with the Quarto de Hóspedes and, along a passage sheltered by a wall running along the courtyard, with

73. The terrace of the
Sala da Audiência or
Council Room, with the
backdrop of the Castelo
dos Mouros standing on
one of the Serra de
Sintra's peaks

74. Central Courtyard:
in the background the
small porch that links
the Sala dos Cisnes and
the Sala das Pegas and
also gives them access
to the Central Courtyard

75. Gruta dos Banhos:
Manueline capital on the
entrance portico

76. Central Courtyard:
decorative mask

the kitchen. On the opposite side, an identical building conceals another spiral staircase, from the period of Dom Manuel I, allowing direct access from this Pátio Central to either the Sala das Sereias or the Sala dos Árabes. Finally, hidden beneath the water tank running along the Sala dos Cisnes, a narrow corridor, with windows giving onto the external portico and lit by cannon-windows on the side of the Pátio Central, formerly gave access to the Sala dos Archeiros and the kitchen (today it only opens onto the external staircase of the palace entrance). This corridor still has its original flooring of Hispano-Arab *azulejos* punctuating the red brick, which is very fine, although worn.

All these internal passages, centring on the Pátio Central, postdate Dom João I, but this does not detract in any way from the area's original function, which was to define the whole group of palace buildings. The subsequent need for better internal access, visible in the construction of various flights of stairs and corridors, has served only to enhance this function.

77. Interior of the first compartment in the Gruta dos Banhos, with eighteenth-century glazed tile compositions

78. Gruta dos Banhos, in the Central Courtyard: the windows of the Sala dos Cisnes can be seen in the background

79. Compartment in the Gruta dos Banhos

80. Doorway between the
Sala das Pegas and the
Sala das Sereias

81. Detail of the ceiling of
the Sala das Pegas

SALA DAS PEGAS

Turning once more to the porch, we enter the first room of the palace, the Sala das Pegas (Magpie Room). Curiously, this is the only room that still has its original name, since this was the name used by Dom Duarte when writing in the early fifteenth century. As with the Sala dos Cisnes (and also the Sala das Sereias), the name derives from the decoration painted on the ceiling: 136 magpies, each holding in its beak a shield with the motto of Dom João I – '*Por bem*' ('In honour') – and, in one of its feet, a rose. The legend associated with this (which the Conde de Sabugosa repeats in his book) relates to an amorous episode involving Dom João I and a lady-in-waiting to the queen, Philippa of Lancaster. (Philippa, the eldest daughter of John of Gaunt, married the Portuguese king in 1387). The tale is probably a much more recent invention, since neither the ceiling nor its pictorial decoration are medieval. In any case, the major restoration work following the earthquake of 1755 repeated the theme of the magpies that is likely to have been there before the disaster in its present or some other form.

According to Dom Duarte's definition of a palace's functions, this was the antechamber where the king received dignitaries of the kingdom and foreign ambassadors. Its airy dimensions allowed the king to present himself in his full authority in surroundings that would have been considered fitting for a man of his rank.

It was customary during medieval times for the monarch to take his day-to-day meals in the antechamber. Furthermore, and once more taking our evidence from the Conde de Sabugosa, it was in this Sala das Pegas that Dom Luis I gave a banquet in honour of the explorers of the African continent, Hermenegildo Capelo and Roberto Ivens, in 1885.

The *azulejos* that decorate the walls and surround the windows and doorways are Hispano-Arab examples dating from the early sixteenth century. With geometric designs in a large format, they accentuate, in dull hues lit up by occasional flashes of light, the majestic functions of this room. The current location and arrangement of these *azulejos* is, however, the result of various changes, particularly following the earthquake of 1755, since both the walls and ceiling had to be restored as a result of this cataclysm.

A fine Renaissance-style fireplace in carved delicate pink marble is set into one of the walls. According to various historical sources, this was brought in the eighteenth century, on the orders of the Dom José's chief minister, the Marquês de Pombal (1699–1782), from the Royal Palace of Almeirim, which no longer exists.

SALA DE DOM SEBASTIÃO

The name of this room comes from its use, according to some historians, as a bedchamber by Dom Sebastião (1554–78) when he was at Sintra. Curiously, the Conde de Sabugosa makes no reference to this circumstance, but simply refers to it as the Sala de Jantar (Dining Room), as this was its use in the time of the last kings of Portugal.

In the description of the palace at Sintra given by Dom Duarte (see *Livro dos Conselhos de el-rei D. Duarte*) this room was called the Câmara de Ouro (Chamber of Gold), perhaps because the decoration on the ceiling or lining the walls was originally in various shades of gold. Indeed, during the reign of Dom Manuel I, many of the palace rooms were known for their gold decoration, to judge by a curious assertion by the viceroy of India, Afonso de Albuquerque (*c.*1462–1515), in a letter written to the king, in which he says that there is more gold and blue in Malacca than in the whole of the palace at Sintra. It may be possible to confirm this assertion shortly through the research work that is being conducted by Rui Trindade and which, when it is concluded, will provide essential information relating to the *azulejos* and ceramics in the National Palace of Sintra (and in Portugal as a whole).

The glazed tile decoration, although using tiles of a larger format, consists of the same naturalistic motifs of vine-leaves in relief that the visitor has already seen in the Sala dos Archeiros. The coping of the ashlar stones consists, however, of a border of cut-out *azulejos* depicting ears of corn in fleur-de-lis form, of highly decorative and technical originality. The doors are similarly outlined with rectangular compositions of *azulejos* in geometric designs, giving a clear visual indication of the communications with adjoining rooms. The observant visitor will notice on the moulding of one of the windows some *azulejos* depicting the armillary sphere (the personal emblem of Dom Manuel I), a circumstance that once again reinforces the different periods of work that went into installing these ceramic panels, which are to be found more or less everywhere in the palace at Sintra.

84. Doorway of the Sala
das Sereias, framed by one
of the most original glazed
tile compositions of the
whole palace

SALA DAS SEREIAS

From the Sala de Dom Sebastião we pass through another small door with a pointed arch into one of the smallest compartments of this part of the palace, known as the Sala das Sereias (Mermaid Room). This relatively recent name relates to the painting on the ceiling, which shows these mythological beings playing various musical instruments and, in the centre, a ship with the Portuguese coat of arms. The painting probably dates from the eighteenth century and is, curiously, almost the same as one decorating the ceiling of a room in the Torre de Ribafria (on the outskirts of Sintra).

According to Dom Duarte's description, the Sala das Sereias was the dressing room serving the nearby rooms. The thickness of its walls and its square plan suggest that it may be a surviving part of a turret of the original Moorish fortress, integrated into the palace built by Dom João I.

The most impressive aspect of this small room is the original *azulejos* on its walls (restored in the eighteenth century), depicting highly naturalistic vine leaves in relief, similar to those in the Sala de Dom Sebastião but smaller in size. These *azulejos* are significant indicators of the change of style and the development of ceramic and tile production techniques in the early sixteenth century. On one of the doors, furthermore, the glazed tile sgraffito is one of the most original in the whole palace, not only for the delicacy of its design but also for the technical skill in its execution. Crowning the glazed tile compositions on all the walls are vases in cut *azulejos* in a strong green colour. These, once again, will have been not only installed but also made (albeit from older *azulejos*) in the second half of the eighteenth century.

In the Sala das Sereias one rectangular doorway, made of white marble, stands out from all the others. It leads to a spiral staircase that connects the Pátio Central to the nearby Sala dos Árabes. On the one hand, this door clearly shows the various alterations that these rooms underwent during the fifteenth and sixteenth centuries to provide new and more convenient means of circulation; on the other hand it can be deduced that the Sala das Sereias would not originally have had as many doors in its walls as the four that are there today. Its specific function as dressing room, with limited access, would not be in accordance with the openness provided by the present doors on all sides. It is likely that only the door communicating with the Sala de Dom Sebastião existed, thus guaranteeing the intimacy of this room.

This is the door through which the visitor is invited to proceed. At the top of the aforementioned spiral staircase is a small but highly original iron dragon, which stands at the end of a screen of the same metal. It is an unusual detail that, in some way, serves to alert the unprepared visitor to the room he or she is about to enter. The crest of the Portuguese royal coat of arms, a mythical animal spitting fire from its mouth, makes it the ancestral guardian of impenetrable spaces, here it is standing guard over the secret Sala dos Árabes, one of the pivotal spaces of the whole royal residence.

SALA DOS ÁRABES

A quadrangular space with a very large window – identical to those in the Sala dos Cisnes – looking out over the Pátio Central, this building had a tall tower above it, as is shown in the drawing by Duarte de Armas from the early sixteenth century. Destroyed by the 1755 earthquake, this strong military tower had afforded the palace at Sintra a fortified appearance that such medieval residences had not yet entirely dared to abandon.

According to the description of the palace by Dom Duarte, this room was used as a bedchamber by his father, Dom João I: it was the 'casa onde el rey que deus perdoe soya dormir' ('the house where the king that God forgives used to sleep'). In any palace or residence of the nobility, this chamber would be the most intimate room of all, so only those closest to the master of the house had access to it. For this reason the fabulous dragon takes on even more symbolic force, standing as it does at the entrance to this space.

In the specific case of the Sala dos Árabes, not only was this room relatively isolated from the rest of the residence, but it was also protected by the powerful military tower that stood above it – both good reasons for it to be chosen as the king's bedchamber, especially since it had an interior room (the room known today as the Quarto de Hóspedes).

The present name of Sala dos Árabes (Arab Room) only dates back to the eighteenth century and relates to the delicate and original fountain in the centre of the floor. Set in a square of polychrome ceramic pieces, geometric in outline and one of the oldest remaining in the palace, this fountain consists of a white marble basin, standing in a circle also of marble and slightly sunken into the floor. The water flowed in fine trickles from the gilded bronze sculpture depicting, on three successive levels, Neptune armed with his trident, putti on the backs of swans alternating with mermaids, and, at the top, an artichoke. The water flowed delicately from the mouths of these putti and from the breasts of the mermaids, introducing a discreet but lively note of sensuality and eroticism to the room.

The Renaissance subjects of the fountain, combined with the cut-out shapes of the basin, show it to be a work from the period of Dom Manuel I, who, as we have already stated, was responsible for the extension and major alterations to the palace at Sintra. The opinion, sustained by some historians, that this fountain was a survival from the original Moorish palace is clearly inconsistent and lacking in any historical basis.

While the doors of the Sala dos Árabes are emphasized, in their outlines, by Hispano-Moorish *azulejos* forming mouldings that isolate them, the walls are lined half-way up with *azulejos* in which the parallelepiped shapes produced by the three colours used (white, green and blue) give rise to different perspectives. These, by their constant shifting, surprise the gaze of the onlooker, amplifying the very space and making it unstable and dynamic. In terms of the effects achieved, this is one of the most spectacular applications of glazed tile compositions in the whole of the palace.

85. Fountain in the floor
of the Sala dos Árabes

86. Sala dos Árabes

87. Sculptural group on
the fountain

QUARTO DE HÓSPEDES

This room originally communicated only with the Sala dos Árabes. The other door that today leads to the kitchen and the highest level of the palace is an addition by Raúl Lino, in imitation Manueline style. Although this has facilitated communication it has destroyed the sense of order of the spaces of a medieval palace, since this room was the inner room of the building erected by Dom João I. As the final space in the exemplary order of a manorial residence, it was the place where the master of the house dressed and undressed, and led only to the bedchamber.

The Quarto de Hóspedes was probably one of the most seriously damaged rooms after the 1755 earthquake. Possibly affected by the collapse of the tower that stood over the Sala dos Árabes, nothing of its original appearance remains apart from the space itself, leaving only the splendid furniture that is exhibited in it worthy of attention. As with practically all the other furniture and objects exhibited in the palace, this has been brought here from other collections (or acquisitions) of the Portuguese state.

Formerly, the Quarto de Hóspedes had a terrace above it that led towards the kitchens and that served to extend the room into the tower above the Sala dos Árabes. Both the terrace and the tower were irremediably damaged by the much-mentioned earthquake in the eighteenth century, and subsequent restorers have set aside any idea of reconstructing them.

88. The Quarto dos
Hóspedes, former interior
room of the Dom João
palace, one of the rooms
most badly affected by the
1755 earthquake

89. Detail of a doorway of
the Sala dos Arabes, showing the *azulejos* used in
decorating the walls. The
tile work is some of the
finest in the palace

90. Pátio da Carranca

PÁTIO DA CARRANCA

Returning to the Sala dos Árabes (to respect the true direction of circulation of the medieval palace) the visitor is invited to descend a staircase that takes him or her to a set of three rooms in the Dom João Building. Halfway there, a landing affords a glimpse of another small inner courtyard, on whose end wall there is a *carranca* or stone face, trickling water into a basin and giving this space its name: the Pátio da Carranca. An opportunity skilfully taken to introduce a further note of freshness through the presence of water, this courtyard is notable for the thick rope moulding that serves as a border to the pool and that is joined at the centre in a knot, and especially for the *azulejos* decorated with the armillary sphere, the personal emblem of Dom Manuel I. Although they have been relocat- ed here from other, almost certainly more noble areas of the palace, these *azulejos* reveal a specific commission by the king to the potteries of Seville, or perhaps more likely to Portuguese potteries which, as the study of Rui Trindade will be able to show, already had the technological capacity to make such items.

91. Whimsical decoration of a window overlooking the Pátio de Diana

92. Sala da Coroa: detail of the Hispano-Arabic tile wall covering

SALA DA COROA

At the end of these stairs, the visitor comes to three rooms whose original purpose has been totally transformed today. The first one, in spite of the ostentatious name, Casa da Coroa (Crown House), by which it is now known (for the royal coat of arms on the ceiling), was part, along with the other small room next to it, of the areas reserved for services to the occupants of this medieval residence. In fact, if we follow the description of the palace given by Dom Duarte (see *Livro dos Conselhos de el-rei D. Duarte*) carefully, it was here that a 'privy' was located and, next to it, '*a casinha de rezar que tem o mijatorio*' (the little house of prayer that contains the urinal). In addition to the evidence of the existence of such places in royal residences, intended to meet basic physiological needs (and, therefore evidence of the degree of hygiene and comfort attained), it is still surprising to have the little house of prayer associated with the meeting of these needs. It is a sense of intimacy that, while it differs from our modern sensibilities, is in fact very consistent with the medieval perception of the body as a source of sinful pleasure, whose natural needs had therefore to be sublimated by means of secluded prayer.

SALA DE CÉSAR

From the Sala da Coroa, the former 'privy', the visitor enters a larger room that has also undergone significant changes. Known today as the Sala de César (Caesar's Room), from the subject of the sixteenth-century Flemish tapestry that is hanging here, it was used as a pantry to the dining room in the final period of the monarchy.

On this part of the tour, the visitor is now familiar with the nucleus of buildings constructed by Dom João I and the logic of their arrangement; in other words, not only do the rooms visited form an entirely independent palace, in terms of their medieval layout, but they also represent, as a whole, the most substantial and characteristic part of the National Palace of Sintra. All that remains to complete this Dom João nucleus is the kitchen. For reasons of convenience, however, the visit to this room will be left to a different part of the tour proposed here.

93. Portuguese galleon
painted on the ceiling of
the Sala das Galés

94. Detail of the entrance
doorway of the Sala dos
Brasões

PÁTIO DE DIANA

Leaving the Sala de César, the visitor passes through a small courtyard, the Pátio de Diana, so-called
because of a statue related to that goddess decorating the central mirror of a double staircase that
gives access to the Sala das Galés. The façade of this room ends in a classical pediment that dates it
to the second half of the sixteenth century or possibly the early seventeenth century.

    The walls of the Pátio de Diana are decorated with *azulejos*, some of which are among the rarest
in the whole palace. As in other places, they were applied here during restorations carried out at various times, having been taken from other parts of the building.

    From this courtyard it is possible to descend to the Pátio do Leão (Lion Courtyard) and then leave
the palace via the Jardim da Preta. But this is not the route we are following. From the Pátio de
Diana, the visitor is invited to enter the Sala das Galés.

SALA DAS GALÉS

The Sala das Galés is a long and narrow rectangular room, forming an independent building from the rest of the palace. It was probably built in the seventeenth century. Standing in an area former-ly occupied only by gardens, this annex relates to these gardens, as well as to the view it offers of the mountainous confines of Sintra. It also has the added curiosity that, on its rounded wooden ceiling, there are depictions of maritime cities and of various ships, whose unfurled flags reveal them to be Portuguese, Dutch and Turkish. According to the Conde de Sabugosa we have at the far end the depiction of an overseas city (possibly Ceuta in North Africa, or an Indian city). In any case, this room is interesting more for the originality of these naval representations than for their artistic merit.

From the Sala das Galés we go up a wooden spiral staircase to the highest and most secluded part of the National Palace of Sintra. The rooms that the visitor passes through at the top, although they do not provide any historical references, do enable us to see the importance of the gardens (especially the Jardim de Lindaraia or Jardim do Príncipe) in the design of the palace, which gradu-ally take possession of the landscape as it unfolds and broadens out. After going down a corridor, we come to the entrance to the Sala dos Brasões on the left.

SALA DOS BRASÕES

The small door that leads into the Sala dos Brasões, sculpted with the twisted designs and bulbous decoration characteristic of Manueline art, immediately intimates to us who was responsible for the decoration of this room, which was built on the site where the Sala da Meca (the name recorded on the drawing by Duarte de Armas) used to be: Dom Manuel I.

The small dimensions of this door add to the surprise that awaits the visitor as he or she crosses the threshold: a vast quadrangular hall almost 13 m long, topped by a very tall dome (13.59 m high) with an octagonal base, on which a great many coats of arms shine with gilded moulding. In the centre, resplendent in gold on a sky blue background, is the coat of arms of Dom Manuel I; around it, those of eight princes and princesses, his children; finally, separated by a band of giant galloping deer, inscribed in octagons, are the heraldic shields of 72 families of the Portuguese nobility.

This magnificent glorification of the person of the monarch transforms a space encircled with some mystery into what is almost a temple to the nobility. While the geometric forms used – the square and the octagon – are synonymous with perfection and ideal beauty (amplified by the room's strict orientation according to the cardinal points), the heraldic decoration embodies, in a tangible way, the centralization of power and the absolutism of the state, attained in the early sixteenth century by the lucid and decisive action of Dom Manuel I. Like a sun, the king shines at the top of the dome; around him, encircled with light but arranged in a meek and orderly fashion, are the loyal and valiant nobles, his subjects.

For this is a gigantic illuminated illustration, unique in Europe, from a *Golden Book of the Nobility*, or a genuine treatise on power and government by the prince, inscribed on the dome of the Sala dos Brasões. The very *azulejos* that decorate the walls (once more, having undergone subsequent rearrangement and restoration, and depicting, in hues of deep blue, scenes of chivalry and hunting), serve not only to highlight the brightness of the gilding on the ceiling but also to enhance the luminous image of the first and foremost class of the kingdom.

So in the interior of the Sala dos Brasões we find one of the crowning monuments underlining the fascination exerted by the National Palace of Sintra: in the literal sense of the word, because it is at the highest point of the acropolis; in the figurative sense, because it is an ambiguous space, between the sacred and the profane – a place of initiation where we are given a glimpse of the luminous and irresistible attraction of power.

Having reached, as we have said, the highest point of the palace, all that remains for the visitor to do is to leave the Sala dos Brasões and make his or her way back down. Returning to the corridor and continuing forwards, we go through the Quarto de Dom Afonso VI and the Sala Chinesa, spaces that make up the oldest part of the palace. In spite of being much transformed, they are presumed to occupy the site of the original ancient palace of the Moorish fortress.

95. Hunting scene in glazed tiles on the walls of the Sala dos Brasões

96. Sala dos Brasões

97. Quarto de Dom Afonso VI

98. Palace chapel

99. Detail of the ceramic
floor of the Quarto de Dom
Afonso VI

QUARTO DE DOM AFONSO VI

Set in between two small rooms, possibly resulting from the alterations made in the reign of Dom
Manuel I (for the purpose of creating an access corridor to the Sala dos Brasões), we find the
Quarto de Dom Afonso VI (1643–83), so named because according to tradition it is here that this
king spent the final years of his life in captivity.

   The most important aspect of this room is its ceramic floor. In spite of serious wear (caused,
legend has it, by the still resounding steps of the poor dethroned monarch), the floor's originality
shines through, its only parallel being the similar floor of the palace chapel. Both of these floors are
still the objects of some controversy among academics, and there are even those who have claimed
that they are authentic vestiges of the original Moorish palace.

   This hypothesis has no historical or artistic basis, however; both of these enamelled ceramic
floors were probably laid during the work undertaken by Dom Afonso V in the second half of the
fifteenth century. Furthermore, they are evidence of the quality and comfort that was being introduced into palaces in the late Middle Ages, in Europe as a whole, with transformations whose scope
we are prevented from understanding better because the majority of them have disappeared or
been remodelled. However, the Museu Nacional Machado de Castro in Coimbra has in its collec-
tion various pieces of coloured ceramic in geometric compositions from the Paço Joanino de Leiria,
which clearly demonstrate the change in palace tastes that has one of its most well-known manifestations in the elegance of these highly elaborate and durable floors.

   The variety of models, patterns, colours and techniques of this floor in the Quarto de Dom
Afonso VI, transform it into an extremely rich and unusual showcase for the glazed tile work of
Portugal and the Iberian Peninsula as a whole.

SALA CHINESA

Leaving the Quarto de Dom Afonso VI the visitor enters the Sala Chinesa (Chinese Room). This room owes its prosaic name to the magnificent miniature of a Chinese pagoda that it contains, an item that was probably given to Dona Maria I by Macao. Nothing else worthy of mention remains in this room.

More important is the historic fact of its having served as a bedchamber for Dom João I, before the monarch extended his royal residence with all the other sections we have already described and visited. Our certainty over the original function of the Sala Chinesa is based, once again, on the invaluable testimony provided by the description of the palace at Sintra given by Dom Duarte (see *Livro dos Conselhos de el-rei D. Duarte*): it is the 'Chamber next to the Chapel where the king slept'. The space occupied by this room in the descriptive sequence of the palace given by Dom Duarte and the measurements that he indicates coincide fully with the area of the Sala Chinesa, leaving us no room for doubt that this was the bedchamber of Dom João I.

This confirmation also adds force to the view that this is the oldest part of the palace, the original centre of the Moorish palace, and again supports our certainty of its original siting and layout.

From the Sala Chinesa the visitor can enter the chapel gallery. However, another proposition is to go down a few steps back to the Sala dos Árabes – the *new* bedchamber of Dom João I – and then to take another staircase down to the inner courtyard of the chapel. Fitting snugly between the Sala dos Árabes, the kitchens – with their imposing chimneys – and a beautiful grand Manueline window that is unique in the whole palace in the modelling of its design and in its decoration, this courtyard allows us to appreciate the large and completely unadorned chapel windows that give an impression of bareness that is completely belied by the interior.

CHAPEL

Built, as everything leads us to believe, by Dom Dinis, the chapel of the National Palace of Sintra is a relatively large space, rectangular in shape, divided transversely by a not very prominent transept that separates the nave from the chancel.

During the reign of Dom Afonso V, this area was deepened to house a new altar, which also led to the penetration of the rear wall of the chancel into one of the kitchen chimneys. In addition to the architectural evidence, we can be certain of this by comparison with the measurements given by Dom Duarte in his description of the palace, which do not include, in relation to the chapel as a whole, this enlargement. Finally, if any doubts remain as to this being the work of Dom Afonso V, the small quadrangular windows installed in this extension (although only one of them is original) are entirely filled with artistic features characteristic of the flamboyant period of Gothic art, contrasting with the already noted decorative simplicity of the large pointed-arch windows in the sides of the transept and the walls of the chancel, which are pointers to the Gothic art of the early fourteenth century, when Dom Dinis reigned in Portugal.

The artistic importance of this medieval palace chapel, highly distinctive in the panoply of Portuguese art, is primarily the result of its being almost the only survivor of the many that existed. The only similar one is the chapel of the University of Coimbra, which once was part of the royal palaces that existed in that city and which was also the subject of a great deal of remodelling in the reign of Dom Manuel I. The Sintra chapel, however, is particularly distinguished for the ceramic paving that still remains on the chancel floor and for its Moorish carved wooden ceiling.

The paved ceramic floor is made up of *alicatados* (a tile-making technique consisting of cutting already painted clay with a file and fitting the pieces together) of various colours, composing Moorish-style geometric designs and imitating a polychrome carpet spread on the floor. It is likely to have belonged to the reign of Dom Afonso V, as, together with the similar composition in the room known as the Quarto de Dom Afonso VI (as we pointed out), it is one of the oldest existing examples in the whole country.

The chapel ceiling is also representative and has the clearly defined characteristics of Moorish art, among the so-called ceilings of *alfarge* or 'knotwork', very common throughout almost all of the Iberian Peninsula. In the specific case of continental Portugal and the island of Madeira, there are several examples of similar ceilings, although the one in the Sintra chapel is, overall, the richest and most elaborate in the variety of its designs and the chromatic richness that resonates throughout the entire composition. All these ceilings (of which the Sintra one is part) correspond, in the end, to a fashion that emerged with great force in Portugal during the fifteenth century (particularly towards its end) and remained throughout the whole of the sixteenth century.

The Moorish ceiling of the National Palace of Sintra chapel was probably commissioned by Dom

Afonso V, following other work carried out in that room that included, in addition to the aforementioned lowering of the chancel, the installation of an altarpiece (unfortunately no longer there, as we have already mentioned) made by the royal painter Nuno Gonçalves and for which he received payment, in 1470, of 23,000 *reals*. The knotwork has been attributed to Dom João I, those supporting this idea using the existence of the João coat of arms on the ceiling as evidence. But that is to forget that the royal coat of arms superimposed on the cross of Avis, the use of which had been initiated by Dom João I, was current up to 1482, in the reign of João II, so it was also used in the same form by Dom Afonso V.

The fresco paintings on all the chapel walls, in spite of being a work of restoration carried out entirely in 1939 (a time when other features of the chapel were removed, such as the carving of the chancel and a gallery in the presbytery area), are based on vestiges of the original decoration, visible at the back of the chancel and over the altar on the left-hand side of the transept. The subject is an endless number of fluttering white doves on a background of strong pink, each with an olive branch in its beak, isolated into squares arranged in a diagonal. As symbols of the Holy Spirit, these doves seem to play on the theme of Pentecost used in the altarpiece commissioned from Nuno Gonçalves. However, in the depiction here, the strongest reference is to the dove that returned to Noah's ark with the olive branch at the end of the flood, symbolizing, in this case, the renewal of the alliance of God with a humanity purified by the regenerative power of water, an episode that, in its turn, prefigures and anticipates Christian baptism.

In any case, and bearing in mind both the artistic and symbolic data, everything points to the fresco painting on the walls of the chapel having also been commissioned by Dom Afonso V. As we have already mentioned, the emotional link felt by this king for the palace at Sintra is well known, it being the place where he was born and died, and on which he lavished particular attention and care. He was also particularly interested in reorganizing the structure and practices of the chapel of the kings of Portugal, and endeavoured to replicate the worship practices of the chapel of the English monarchy. The extension of the chancel of Sintra and the ceramic paving of its floor, the installation of the Moorish ceilings and, finally, the complete painting of the walls in fresco, consolidate and give concrete expression to these concerns of Dom Afonso V, who was eager for his court to be compared, in the radiance and grandeur of its palaces and their chapels, with those of other European monarchs.

The chapel of the National Palace of Sintra, in spite of the restorations carried out at various periods, is one of the most well-preserved medieval spaces in Portugal, and therefore most representative of the artistic sensibilities of the late Middle Ages. Elements of Islamic art, present in the *alfarge* ceilings and in the *alicatado* flooring, are combined with European fresco painting in an area

intended for reflection and the experience of the Christian religion. Interestingly, those creating the chapel did not hesitate to use artistic elements from a religious and cultural world that was different from their own.

There is no doubt that, in the National Palace of Sintra as a whole, the ever-present appeal of this remote Moorish past finds in its chapel one of its most evident and even striking manifestations.

After viewing the chapel it is time for the visitor to enter the final room, which, together with the chapel and the Sala dos Brasões, is one of the most exuberant and characteristic spaces in the National Palace of Sintra. We refer of course to the kitchen, which the visitor now reaches by two new flights of stairs.

102. Palace chapel ceiling

103. Palace kitchen

KITCHEN

We enter this large rectangular area through a modest door with straight lintels, but the original entrance, a pointed-arch door, can still be seen closed up in the wall.

The monumental kitchen is divided down the middle by a wide pointed arch. It is lit by small double windows, also with pointed arches, that are located on the east side, as well as by several other small windows set in the two chimneys.

It is these conical chimneys, each approximately 33 m high, that give the room its greatest originality. Forming the ceiling of the kitchen, they are quite unique – in their double form and in their dimensions – in the whole of Europe. Although there are a few chimneys to be found in European abbeys or palaces that are similar to those of Sintra in terms of their size and grandeur, none outside the country has the same structure as those in the Portuguese palace.

It is probable that other palaces in Portugal had double chimneys that were similar in style. Indeed, examples remain in the Palácio da Independéncia, in Lisbon, but their diminutive scale, however elegant, makes them almost a toy in comparison with the gigantic size of the Sintra chimneys. As a consequence the latter have come to be emblematic of the palace as a whole and indeed of Sintra itself.

The kitchen was built by Dom João I and its unusual dimensions clearly affirm one of its primary functions – to prepare for the table the abundant supply of game for which the Serra was famed. As we have already mentioned, the king was so passionate about this sport of the nobility that he wrote a treatise on the physical and moral virtues of hunting.

The lining of the interior walls of the kitchen in white *azulejos* dates from the late nineteenth century, although the large heraldic composition of the royal coat of arms of Portugal and the Casa de Sabóia belongs to the time of Dona Maria I (Maria Pia). This very grand *azulejo* composition, exemplary in its heraldic significance by being displayed in a utilitarian space in which its colours stand out dramatically from the hygienic white of the walls, is, curiously, a reassertion and formulation of the importance that the dimensions of the Sintra kitchen (and, in the end, of the whole palace) held in the nineteenth-century imagination and mind.

In the corner to our left as we enter, at the side of a service door that gives access both to the lower floor of the kitchen itself and to the Pátio Central, the visitor can catch a glimpse of the rocky outcrop of the massif on which the whole palace is built, giving a clear indication of the solidity of the hill chosen as the site for this royal residence.

Although this is the end of the official tour of the National Palace of Sintra, there are two other spaces that are closed to the public, but which are worth mentioning: the Sala das Duas Irmãs and the Pátio dos Tanquinhos.

SALA DAS DUAS IRMÃS AND PÁTIO DOS TANQUINHOS

Beneath the Sala dos Brasões is a ground-floor room, divided into three bays by two rows of arches supported on columns. In the nineteenth century this was known as the Sala das Duas Irmãs (Room of the Two Sisters), to liken it to the room of the same name in the Alhambra of Granada. It was also called the Sala de Afonso V, after a well-intentioned legend that identified this space as the place where that king was born and died. But the Sala das Colunas (Column Room), as it is more prosaically known today, did not exist during the reign of Dom Afonso V, having only been built by Dom Manuel I, between 1517 and 1518, as a fundamental support for the Sala dos Brasões.

The architectural and sculptural forms of this room are very typical of the art of the Manueline period. They do, however, reveal subsequent work, which is particularly visible in the quadrangular and very high plinth on which all the columns stand. In any case, this circumstance is not sufficient to prevent us from accepting the originality of this space.

The ground-floor Sala das Colunas or Sala das Duas Irmãs is connected to a small walled court-yard – the Pátio dos Tanquinhos – which has already been described in another part of this guide. With its generous windows in the walls and its thoughtfully placed seats, it invites the visitor to take a rest and final look around.

Behind it, partly hidden by the robust elevation of the Sala dos Brasões, we can still glimpse, to the south, the Castelo dos Mouros, built between mighty rocks that dispute with it the desire to out-line, in magical profile, the mountain of Sintra; in front, on clear days, the visitor's gaze is lost in the vast blue of the ocean.

This site at the far end of Europe is a place that encourages peaceful solitude and slow medita-tion; while here, savour the potent words of the internationally renowned novelist and essayist Virgilio Ferreira (1916–96) which, in this very place, feel like the most appropriate cry:

'Sintra is the most beautiful farewell of Europe as it finally reaches the sea . . .'

108. Dom Dinis: detail
of recumbent statue
(Convento de Odivelas)

BIOGRAPHICAL NOTES

DOM DINIS (1261–1325)

Seventh king of Portugal, son of Dom Afonso III and Dona Beatriz of Castile, he assumed the throne in 1279 to begin a long reign of forty-six years. He fought against the privileges that limited his royal authority, especially through the investigations carried out to verify the legitimacy of lands claimed by the aristocracy, initiated in 1284, which allowed many lands usurped from the Crown to be returned. He established a concordat with the Holy See in 1290, bringing to an end a dispute that was dragging on and which also returned to the Portuguese Crown land illegally confiscated by members of the clergy. One of his most successful measures was to prevent the disappearance of the Order of the Knights Templar, re-establishing it as the Order of Christ. Abroad, his most well-known intervention was that of obtaining the reformulation of the lands of Riba-Coa, through the treaty of Alcanizes, which fixed the boundaries of Portugal much as they are today. He achieved much in the fields of internal and external trade, in supporting agriculture, in founding new towns, in the repair of old fortresses or the building of new ones. The founding of the Portuguese University in 1290 kept the country in step with what had become an international movement. A highly cultured man himself, he ordered the translation of major works on history and law, he was among the most important poets of his time and his court one of the most notable literary centres of the Iberian Peninsula. During his reign, Gothic art (and particularly architecture) became established via a set of experiments, abandoning the aesthetics and processes that were still bound by Romanesque art. The building or extension of residential palaces, both for the king himself and for the nobility in general, saw its first great period of expansion during his reign, clearly illustrating the distinctive development represented by the reign of this king in almost every field.

DOM JOÃO (1357–1433)

Tenth king of Portugal, son of Dom Pedro I and a lady from Galicia – Teresa Lourenço. Grand Master of the Order of Avis since his childhood, he was proclaimed king in 1385, following the crisis initiated two years earlier by the death of the reigning monarch, Dom Fernando. The same year he emerged victor, in the fields of Aljubarrota, against the armies of the king of Castile (himself a candidate for the throne of Portugal), thereby consolidating not only his crown but also the country's independence. His reign, after the signing of permanent peace with Castile, was a long period of internal and external peace that not even the conquest of Ceuta (in 1415), precursor of the maritime adventures of the Portuguese, managed to disturb. A man of great culture (perhaps the most learned of all the medieval monarchs and the one best prepared to govern), he was able to create the conditions for the excellent education that his children were to receive and that was behind the literary talent shown by some of them. He ordered the translation of several works into Portuguese

109. Dom Duarte: detail of recumbent statue (Mosteiro de Batalha)

and he himself wrote, after 1415, a *Livro da Montaria*, in which he demonstrated a full knowledge of the techniques of riding and hunting on horseback. He was a great patron of the arts. Although his most well-known act of patronage is the Mosteiro da Batalha (Batalha Abbey) – a work which had considerable impact on the Portuguese and European late-Gothic architectural scene, and one which affirmed his ascent to the throne – he radically extended both the palace at Sintra, providing it with it conditions of comfort that had not existed before, and the Alcáçova of Lisbon, where (when he fell ill in Alcochete) he wished to die. He built other palaces from scratch, including those in Leiria, Muge and Almeirim. It can be said that, with Dom João I, Portuguese art attained the level of the rest of Europe, partly as a result of his policy of unions (including matrimonial ones) with some of the principal houses and, especially, of the internal peace he managed to maintain in a rather turbulent period.

DOM DUARTE (1391–1438)

Eleventh king of Portugal, son of Dom João I and Philippa of Lancaster, he assumed the throne in 1453. Although his father had already involved him in governing, his reign was a very short one, just five years, and it took place under somewhat painful circumstances, interpreted in dramatic form by history and legend. The ill-fated attack on the Moroccan city of Tangier in 1437 was one of the main reasons for the low spirits in which the king ended his days. A man of great culture and given to speculation, he had a rich library, wrote the *Leal Conselheiro* (a treatise on the knowledge of the time), he penned the *Arte de Bem Cabalgar toda a Sela* and left us a set of personal reflections (*Livro dos Conselhos de El-Rei D. Duarte – Livro da Cartuxa*) that provide a valuable testimony to the practices, customs and philosophy of the period. Significant among these notes is the description, with the respective measurements, of the rooms of the palace at Sintra, an invaluable piece of work that enables us to know with some accuracy the layout of this palace in the early fifteenth century, following the major renovations and extensions carried out by Dom João I.

DOM MANUEL I (1469–1521)

Fourteenth king of Portugal, ninth son of Prince Fernando and Dona Brites, he was grandson, on his father's side, of Dom Duarte and great-grandson, on both his father's and his mother's side, of Dom João I. The accident that killed the heir to the throne unexpectedly gave him the crown in 1495, left to him in his will by Dom João II, at the very moment when the country was well on the way to its most spectacular adventure. His reign, which lasted twenty-six years, saw an intense activity in the fields of internal, external and overseas politics. He carried out great institutional reforms of a political and fiscal nature, such as that of charters and legislation (summarized in the Manueline Ordinances), always with a view to strengthening and centralizing royal power. It was during his reign that Vasco da Gama reached India and Pedro Álvares Cabral arrived in Brazil, bringing about

110. Dom Manuel with St Jerónimo: statue on the main entrance to the Mosteiro dos Jéronimos, Lisbon

the domination of the East. He maintained a foreign policy as active as it was cautious, avoiding the various European conflicts of the time while asserting (and consolidating at the same time) his power and prestige. A great patron and supporter of all the arts, his reign was distinguished not only by the number and quality of works of art of all kinds produced in the country or imported, but also by a style so powerful and original that historiography gave it the name Manueline art. Closely accompanying the assertion of European late Gothic style, Manueline art in fact has many very unusual characteristics that justify its own label. The Mosteiro dos Jerónimos and the Torre de Belém in Lisbon, and the refurbishment and extension of the Convento de Cristo at Tomar are outstanding in the field of architecture. In the National Palace of Sintra, his intervention can be seen not only in the construction of a new wing and the emblematic Sala dos Brasões but also in the refurbishment and extension of the existing buildings in such a way that the essential image of the building is, even today, shot through with this intervention.

BIBLIOGRAPHY

Amaro, Clementino, 'Silos Medievais no Palácio Nacional de Sintra', *Arqueologia Medieval*, Campo Arqueológico de Mértola/Ed. Afrontamento, Lisbon, 1992.

Armas, Duarte de, *Livro das Fortalezas*, Lisbon, ANTT-INAPPA, 1990 [facsimile ed. of Ms. 159 of the Casa Forte do Arquivo Nacional da Torre do Rombo].

Barbosa, Inácio Vilhena, 'Palacio Real de Sintra', *Archivo Pittoresco*, vol. VII, 1864.

Coelho, A. Borges, *Portugal na Espanha Árabe*, 4 vols, Lisbon, Seara Nova, 1971–4.

Correia, Ana Maria Arez R. E. B., *Palacio Nacional de Sintra*, Lisbon, Elo, 1993.

Costa, Francisco, *O Paço Real de Sintra. Novos Subsídios para a sua História*, Sintra, Câmara Municipal, 1980.

Dom Duarte, *Leal Conselheiro*, (critical and annotated ed. by J.-M. Piel), Lisbon, Livrª. Bertrand, 1942.

Dom Duarte, *Livro dos Conselhos de el-rei D. Duarte (Livro da Cartuxa)* (diplomatic edition and transcription by J. J. Alves Dias), Lisbon, Ed. Estampa, 1982.

Freire, Anselmo Braamcamp, *Brasões da Sala de Sintra*, 2nd ed., Coimbra, Imprensa da Universidade, 1921.

Góis, Damião de, *Crónica do Felicíssimo Rei D. Manuel*, Part I, Coimbra, Imprensa da Universidade, 1926.

Góis, Damião de, *Descrição da Cidade de Lisboa* (translation of the Latin text, introduction and notes by J. Felicidade Alves), Lisbon, Livros Horizonte, 1988.

Haupt, Albrecht, *A Arquitectura do Renascimento em Portugal*, Lisbon, Ed. Presença, 1985.

Juromenha, Visconde de, *Cintra Pinturesca*, Lisboa, 1838.

Lino, Raúl, 'O Paço Real de Sintra', in *Palácios Portugeses*, vol. 1, Lisbon, 1973.

Lino Raúl, *Quatro Palavras sobre os Paços Reais de Sintra*, Lisbon, Valentim de Carvalho, 1948.

Pérez Embid, F., *El Mudejarismo en la Arquitectura de la Epoca Manuelina*, Seville, 1944.

Sabugosa, Conde de, *O Paço de Sintra*, Lisbon, Imprensa Nacional, 1903.

Serrão, Vítor, *Sintra*, Lisbon, Ed. Presença, 1989.

Silva, José Custódio Vieira da, *Paços Medievais Portugueses*, Lisbon, IPPAR, 1995.

Silva, José Custódio Vieira da, 'Il Tardogotico nell'Architettura Civile Portoghese (XV–XVI secolo)', *L'Architettura del Tardogotico in Europa*, Milan, Guerini e Ass., 1995.

Silva, José Custódio Vieira da, 'Palácio Nacional de Sintra', *Sintra Património da Humanidade*, Sintra, Câmara Municipal, 1996.

Silva, José Custódio Vieira da, 'Palácio Nacional de Sintra: o poder de um lugar, séculos XV a XIX', *Lugares de Poder. Europa Séculos XV a XX*, Lisbon, Fundação Calouste Gulbenkian, 1998.

Souza, A. D. de Castro e, *Descripção do Palácio Real da Villa de Cintra*, Lisbon, 1838.

INDEX